AN UNEXPECTED HOPE

AN
UNEXPECTED HOPE

Finding Satisfaction
When Life Disappoints

ROGER C. PALMS

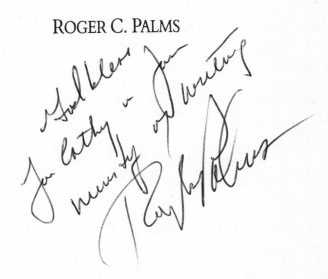

CROSSWAY BOOKS • WHEATON, ILLINOIS
A DIVISION OF GOOD NEWS PUBLISHERS

CONTENTS

PREFACE

Disappointments, sorrows, the end of a dream—we all face these. Dead ends, walls we can't seem to climb over. The sharp edges, the pains of life sometimes threaten to overwhelm us. And we cry out, "What is God doing?"

God doesn't have to answer us, of course, but usually he does, either at that moment or later. It is then that we say with overwhelming awe, "Look at what God has done with this that seemed so horrible to me."

In the economy of God, we find that he wastes nothing. From what seems the darkest of nights he often brings the brightest of dawns.

In these pages I've opened my life to you. I've tried to be as transparent as I can—not for pity or for praise, but in order for you to see God at work in one man's life and the lives of those he loves.

We learn from one another. So perhaps in these pages as you learn about me, you will learn about yourself. I hope so.

And I hope that when you close this book at the last page, you will be able to say with me: "To have God is to have hope. To have God is to have life. To have God is—above all—to have God."

What more could any of us want?

1

A JOURNEY OF FAITH
BEGINS

IT WAS A LITTLE AFTER one in the afternoon. I'd had my lunch—a sandwich. The empty brown bag was now folded and in my briefcase. I'd use that bag again tomorrow. Now at a small carrel in the library of Wayne State University in Detroit, I opened a textbook. I was a sophomore; I needed to study. But I could not. Instead, as happened the night before and the day before that, the pages of my textbook started to blur. At first a few tears came, then more. I couldn't stop; I could only let go and cry. Sobs came wrenching up from pain deep inside.

"Yes, but You're Not"

A few months earlier, through the witness of a friend, I had invited Jesus Christ into my heart. I asked him to be my Savior. I asked him to be my Lord. It wasn't a quick decision nor an easy one. Russ, my friend, had fought a hard battle with me.

Russ and I had gone to the same high school and had worked on the *Mercury*, the school newspaper; we had fun together. But during the summer between high school graduation and the start of college classes, Russ had become a Christian. Since I had a car and he didn't, and we were both commuting students, I'd pick him up every morning, and he'd ride to the university with me. And he talked; he talked about Jesus; he talked about conversion; he talked about new peace, a different joy. He drove me nuts with it.

I don't know if I'd ever met a Christian before. Maybe I had, but I couldn't recall ever listening to one, and now I was in a car with a "fanatic." I did what most people do—I argued. "Look, if you need God, fine. I don't." "If religion helps you, you go ahead and have your religion. I don't need the crutch."

Russ didn't stop talking during that fall and winter as we rode together. Occasionally I'd be curious and ask a question. He was different—I couldn't deny that. There was something about his explanations and the Bible quotes that made sense. It did seem logical that God would do what he said God did, and love as Russ said God loved, and offer new life in Christ as the Scriptures Russ quoted said.

One morning in one of my "I don't want to hear any more" moods, I was driving too fast and, rounding a corner, almost turned the car so it was on two wheels. Russ grabbed the dash with one hand, the door handle with the other, and in those pre-seat belt days, braced his feet and screamed, "Hey, watch it!" He was scared, and I was glad. It was my moment.

"What are you worried about?" I taunted. "You're a Christian."

With a newfound composure Russ turned to me and said quietly but firmly, "Yes, but you're not."

And I couldn't get over that. I couldn't shake those words, "Yes, but you're not." They stayed with me, playing over and over in my mind. "Yes, but you're not." My wall started to break. In time I went with Russ to his church, then to his college-age Sunday school class; and in March of that year, in the home of a businessman who taught that class, I followed the Scriptures he showed me and opened my life to the Savior.

I was a new creation, and I knew it. No one had to tell me; I saw everything in a new light. Scripture became mine; the Bible understood me. Christian music and prayer and new Christian friends ushered me into a world I never dreamed existed.

Maybe I Was Already Crazy

My happiness went beyond anything I had ever known before. A deep sense of peace at the love and security I found in Christ was overwhelming—for a while.

Then the pressures began. I had eagerly told my family that I had met Christ. I guess I thought they would want Christ too. That wasn't their reaction.

I'd hear at home that I was unbalanced, crazy. "Look at you, a religious fanatic," they said. Day after day I heard it. Was it true? Was I so wrong? Was I only convincing myself that God was real, that he loved me?

Sleepless nights, the agony of trying to defend a belief that I had only just come to myself, the confusion of hearing that I was going over the edge—all had their effect.

That day in the library I knew that I could not go on. Maybe they were right. Maybe I was losing my mind. Maybe I was already what they said I was. Maybe I was already crazy. I shut my book and made my decision. "I'll go to the health center and see a staff psychiatrist. There must be something wrong with me."

A Journey of Faith Begins

A Great Washing

Between the third and second floors of that library, there is a stairway landing with a door to the men's restroom. I pushed open the door. *At least I can wash away the tears before I go outside,* I thought.

As I stood by the sink, I realized I was alone. No one else was in there. In a desperation that came from my pain, I cried out, "Oh, God, if you are real, show me."

It had never happened before; it has never happened since, but as I cried out that plea from my heart, it was as though someone slapped me so hard that I actually spun around—*and I knew.* I knew that God was there. A peace flooded over me like a great washing.

I left that restroom, went back upstairs to my studies, and was as a man with a new awareness of reality.

Were all the struggles over? Did all my pain go away? Did the people in my family suddenly embrace my Christian faith? No, but I had an assurance that God is real, that he means what he says. The comfort of "I will never leave you nor forsake you" carried me on—year in and year out.

The time came, later, when one by one each member of my family did come to faith in Christ. The time came when they were supportive of me, but not all at once. I could only hang on to the assurance that God is who he says he is, that he will do what he says he will do, and that he loves me as he said he does.

Now I Knew

Those nights had been long and dark, the pain of uncertainty real, the hurt of being told I was crazy overwhelming. But

Finding Satisfaction When Life Disappoints

now I knew; I was experiencing what Isaiah the prophet himself had learned years before: "When you pass through the waters, I will be with you; and when you pass through the rivers, they will not sweep over you. When you walk through the fire, you will not be burned; the flames will not set you ablaze. For I am the LORD, your God" (Isaiah 43:2-3).

This is a painful life for many of us; we live in a dream world if we think otherwise. We will walk through the waters and the flame—but not alone. Isaiah was a realist. As I came to know pain and more of God in the midst of my pain, I slowly became a realist too. I became one who learned to cling to the promise, "I will be with you."

God is for me; I know that. God loves me, I am sure. And sometimes in the still-rough places, in the ongoing difficult trials, in the tensions and the frustrations and the stresses, that realization is all I have to cling to. This I know: God is for me. I may not know much else, but I know that—God is for me. I think, now, that I can face anything knowing that God is for me.

I Am Protected

God knows what you and I are facing. Those who tell God, "You don't know what I'm going through," are not telling the truth. God does know. We hear that statement again and again from people we want to help. As we start to encourage them, give them our support, they turn on us: "But you don't know what I'm facing," meaning that if we did know, we would realize that no one can help them, not even God. They talk about family pressures, illness, job loss, inability to pay the bills. "You

A Journey of Faith Begins

don't know what I'm facing," they say. And, of course, we don't. No one knows all that you are facing; no one knows all that I am facing. No one, that is, but God.

But I turn to Proverbs. Why? Because I don't have to know all that another person is facing. I know that God knows. He cares and offers a way to his refuge. As a helper of others and as a depender on God myself, I know that "the way of the LORD is a refuge for the righteous" (Proverbs 10:29). And I've discovered the truth of the words that follow: "The righteous will never be uprooted" (Proverbs 10:30).

Though there is a lot to face in this life that will shake you and me, that promise of God is certain: "The righteous will never be uprooted." A right relationship—that's where the protection is. "The way of the LORD is a refuge for the righteous." Have you learned that yet?

I need that refuge. I need a position that will never be uprooted. There are too many situations in which I would be absolutely uprooted by all that is going on around me if I didn't have the refuge of God. The Refuge is always the Refuge. The Protector is always the Protector. The Security is always the Security. God is always God. I am not alone.

God Cares

I once had a friend who proved that every single day. One evening a few years ago, as I sat down at the dinner table, I commented that I didn't recall ever seeing that particular casserole before. My wife, Andrea, replied, "You haven't." Then she explained, "It's Bev's casserole."

Finding Satisfaction When Life Disappoints

But it couldn't be. Bev was in an iron lung; she had been for many years. Then, as we ate, I got the story. Bev, who died not long after this dinner-table conversation, had a lot of hobbies; cooking was one of them. She also had a lot of friends who came to visit her in the nursing facility where she lived. These friends sometimes took dictation as she kept up a voluminous correspondence. Sometimes they wrote checks when it was time for her to pay her bills. Sometimes they played games (which Bev usually won). And they cooked.

Bev would lie there and think about the creation of a new dish, plan it, order the ingredients, and then with the hands of a visitor, the meal was made. Sometimes she invited friends over for a dinner party. Other times she kept portions for herself and her mother or gave some to the nursing home staff (why live on institutional food when you can be creative?), and the cook/helper got to take the rest home. The casserole that evening was delicious.

Bev was a committed Christian with a meaningful prayer life. She had Bible study habits that kept her growing. She had a whole network of friends and was a member of a church even though she could never attend. By phoning, writing, and talking to her visitors (so many people that they had to schedule their hours with her), she encouraged all. And she gave perspective to every life she touched.

Bev and I were about the same age, yet our lives were so different. I had my health, I could walk around, I could have a job and a family. She could have none of that. Bev proved to me that God cares about us. He was her refuge. She had every reason to be angry, bitter, a recluse. She was the opposite. She believed that in spite of her circumstances God was there to help her. And all of us who knew her realized that she had learned a lesson in trust that so many walking around still haven't learned.

Because You Trust

You probably know someone like Bev. You have seen that person rebound even when there are disasters, even when everything seems to be falling apart. That person, like Bev, shows us that even when all of society is suffering, God still knows each of us as individuals. Even in that part of Scripture that shows God's judgment side, we can still see his tender compassion. He warns that he is going to bring disaster on a city; but then he says to a person like you, a person like me, "But I will rescue you on that day . . . you will not be handed over to those you fear. I will save you; you will not fall by the sword but will escape with your life, because you trust in me" (Jeremiah 39:17-18).

That's the key: "Because you trust in me." Whenever I begin to be afraid and start questioning—will I fall? will I suffer? will God deliver me?—I keep coming back to the first question that everyone should ask: Am I trusting him? God makes it clear— no doubts about it, no speculation or guessing: "Because you trust me" (v. 18). "Never mind what's happening around you," he says, in effect. "I will deliver you because you trust me." Since God knows each individual who trusts him, in a world full of confusion and hurt, my responsibility and yours is to be one of those people, the trusting ones.

Are you one of those trusting ones? Are you like Bev? With

Finding Satisfaction When Life Disappoints

me, are you learning how to be that kind of person? We can discover together that there is more for us even when life offers less. In the pages that follow, you and I can learn that God always means what he says and that he does love us very much.

I have discovered over this lifetime Christian journey that I can know that I'm protected when I give myself in trust to the Protector. I can know that I am one of the righteous to whom God offers refuge when in surrender I say to the one who is the way, the truth, the life, "Please forgive my stubborn no's of the past. Please take from me the sin that has separated us for so long." And, with David the psalmist, I have learned to plead, "Create in me a pure heart, O God, and renew a steadfast spirit within me" (Psalm 51:10).

Then I am able to claim the promise: "If we confess our sins, he is faithful and just and will forgive us our sins and purify us from all unrighteousness" (1 John 1:9). Then I can hold in my heart the certainty: "Therefore, there is now no condemnation for those who are in Christ Jesus" (Romans 8:1). Then I can justly claim the assurance God offers: "In the way of righteousness there is life; along that path is immortality" (Proverbs 12:28). Are you claiming that too?

I have learned that God means what he says. Russ taught me; Bev taught me; and in the years since, though I had no idea what was coming, I have learned that God offers more when life offers less. I am learning, and I am watching others learn too that no matter what happens, God has my best interest in his heart.

A Journey of Faith Begins

FOR REFLECTION OR DISCUSSION

1. Are you a new creation in Christ? How do you know?

2. In what special or personal way can you recall God meeting you?

3. What does God's promise, "I will be with you," mean to you?

4. Has there been a "Bev" in your life? What did that person do or say that influenced your life?

2

In My
Best Interest

ROB IS LOOKING FORWARD to the weekend with his family. They have plans that promise a happy two days together. Then at 4:15, just fifteen minutes before his weekend begins, his phone rings.

Cheerfully, he picks up the handset. His supervisor is asking to see him. Quickly he walks down the hall, steps into the large office, and with neither the courtesy of preliminaries nor small talk, his world is shattered.

This middle manager in his early fifties hears the devastating words: "Rob, your job has been eliminated." He is allowed no time to say good-bye to his colleagues, no time to finish a project on his desk, no time to telephone his wife. He must be out of the building by 4:30. Somebody from the security department stands by watching as he packs photographs and other personal items on his desk and credenza. He will be allowed several months' severance, and, if he wants it, on Monday he can return for an hour of out-placement counseling.

There had been no warning, no hint that his termination was coming. Now as he walks from the building and heads to his parking space, he wonders, *What will I say to my wife, my friends, my neighbors?* He is certain that everyone is watching him, as though they see on his forehead a big red letter "R"—Rejected.

Six months later, still looking for work, he has begun to cash

In My Best Interest

in IRAs meant for his retirement, paying the penalty for early use. He struggles with the question of his own worth, his value, and cries in the night, "Does God hate me so much?"

God Doesn't Want to Hurt Me

It is a simple truth, but it is often misunderstood by you, by Rob, and by me: God does not want to hurt us. Why then does it seem as though he does? There is a lot of pain in our world, and some, like Rob, have felt a great deal of it. How do I, how does he, how do any of us make sense of such pain when it overwhelms, strangles, cripples?

I meet others like Rob in many places. One lives on my street; another sits across the aisle in church on Sunday mornings; another does volunteer work in a retirement community. Rob prays, but for him, and others, it is a private pain. Pastors call to ask, "Will you drive our young people to camp?" or, "Can you help with Vacation Bible School?" In the administration of the church program he is seen as an available worker. But his wife knows that his self-image is shattered. No one calls to ask, "How are you getting along?" No one says, "I am praying for you." He doesn't hear, "We love you." And that would help. He doesn't hear, "God loves you," either; and there are days when, if someone did say it, he'd reply under his breath, "I doubt it."

God Loves Me?

But God does love us. For nearly twenty-five years I observed and wrote about the Billy Graham Evangelistic

Finding Satisfaction When Life Disappoints

Crusades around the world. I have heard a lot of Billy Graham's sermons. At first I wondered at the emphasis Mr. Graham always puts on God's love. "God loves you," he always says and then repeats that several times. "He loves you, he loves you, he loves you."

But later as I interviewed counselors who speak to the people who go forward at the invitation to make a personal decision to follow Jesus Christ as Savior and Lord, I heard repeated over and over again the same words. Those who respond to the Gospel exclaim, "I didn't know that God loved me. I always felt alienated from God. I thought that I could never please him. So many bad things have happened in my life, I thought God hated me." I have heard it in Japan, in France, in Brazil, in Kenya. I've heard it in Sweden and in Singapore: "God loves me? I didn't know that."

In Moscow, Russia, one woman, speaking in the language of her Russian Orthodoxy, said, "I knew that the priest could approach God in the cathedral, but now I can approach God too. I have a cathedral in my heart."

And we do. Each one of us does. In our best interest, God has placed a cathedral in our hearts. God is not far away from us. God is near. In love, he stays near us and keeps us. With different words, in different ways, all through the Scriptures, he repeats over and over again, "I love you!" Love is the compelling word that shows through all the other parts of God's Word—"I love you." "I want to bring you back to myself." "I want to live my life in you and for you." "For your best interest, I want to live out my best interest in your life."

In My Best Interest

A New Perspective

This is no contradiction to all the painful things that happen to us. God's best interest is my best interest. And my best interest is his best interest. Our interests are not opposite. We are not in tension with one another. God does not want to be looked at as our antagonist. Because he isn't. He is not here to hurt me but to help me. He is not here to hurt you either. He keeps saying so.

I need that reminder day after day. So does Rob. In the midst of all that happens to me I so easily forget. So does he. And probably so do you.

Yet slowly, not with great flashes of insight but a little at a time, a new perspective is taking hold of Rob. He is not the first, nor will he be the last, to learn what he is learning. As it becomes clear that there won't be another position for him like the last one, he begins to gain perspective. There are occasional jobs, short-term free-lance assignments, an occasional two-week consultation. But no career-enhancing offer, no health benefits, no pension, no title on an office door.

"I can't define myself by what I do, can I?" Rob said one day. "I'm more than a profession. God is showing that to me. My wife and I are poorer now, but I believe we are closer to each other. And I'm finding as I read Scripture, as I pray, that there is a deeper relationship with God than I knew about when I was pushing my own way ahead. There is a lot more to me than I ever knew. God is showing me that. I'd like to be working again, but I wouldn't want to look at life again as I once did."

Finding Satisfaction When Life Disappoints

No Blank Spaces

All of us learn at our own pace—Rob at his, you at yours, me at mine. Slowly, I'm coming to know, on the basis of what God says about himself, that God wants me to be fulfilled. He wants me to be at peace. He wants me to have joy. Not just up and down hilarity but deep-down joy. If God didn't, he wouldn't keep pointing out to you and me that this is what he does want.

I know that I miss out when I try to make my own pleasures or my own satisfaction. I can't ever be to myself what God wants to be to me. I did not make myself. I did not make my world, and I can't make sense of where I fit or don't fit in this world. God alone knows and can bring me to where I need to be and teach me what I need to know.

Jonah learned that. Sloshing around in a fish's belly is a tough place to go to school. But he gained a whole new perspective while he was in there. He didn't ask for the experience, but when the fish finally spat him out on land and he walked to Nineveh in the hot sun smelling like the inside of a fish, he knew that God must really care about him. His importance now was based on the deliverance and call of God.

In a similar way, Moses had his wilderness. So did Paul. Daniel had his prison and John his exile. None wanted it, but none was ever the same again because of it.

A lot of books have been written about our human potential: self-fulfillment books, what-you-can-be type books. Some are about physical satisfaction—you can be thinner, have fewer wrinkles. Some are aimed at the emotions—you can be more aggressive, more in control. And some are vaguely aimed at the spiritual—you can be more like God.

But God's word to you and me is like none of these. It is more! Ephesians 3:19 explains what is ours as a certainty. There the apostle Paul (the beaten, shipwrecked, cast-in-a-dungeon, thrown-out-of-town Paul) says that we can "know this love that surpasses knowledge—that you may be filled to the measure of all the fullness of God."

Filled to "all the fullness of God."

Talk about possibilities! But how do I get that? I can't just ignore what is going on around me. I can't pretend that I don't feel what I feel. I'm not an ostrich with my head in the sand. Neither are you.

Or does this promise come to us not in opposition to reality but in the midst of it?

I think, as I read about Paul who wrote these words, I'm seeing a man who knew that what he was saying would make no sense to people who have not felt pain. Here is a man who knew real pain telling me that I can know a love "that surpasses knowledge." I may be "filled to the measure of all the fullness of God." In other words, filled and filled and filled to "all the fullness of God." Not that I will be all of God—that's impossible—but rather that all that is of God will fill me.

Think of it! No blank spaces. No partial fulfillment. The fullness of God filling me and filling me. Paul knew it because he knew pain. But, more than that, he knew it because he also knew God.

Finding Satisfaction When Life Disappoints

I'm Not a Self-made Person

I think that one reason the market has been so saturated with self-improvement books and magazines dedicated to the self is that each of us is urged to think about "my needs, my wants, my desires, my fulfillment." The focus is on me and who I am. That's what our culture teaches us. But if I have that focus, I will always be focused backwards. Once I learn where the filling comes from and I don't turn away from it, once I know that God cares about my best interest, I can focus on God and let him focus on my best interest.

Unlike what we find in so many bookstores, the Bible is not a self-help book. The Bible is a God-helping-us book. The Bible is a book of love for you and me, but it is not a self-love book. It is good for me from time to time—when I start to think how important I am—to go through Scripture not to look at "all I am" but to look at all of the passages that speak of Christ and who he is: "For God was pleased to have all his fullness dwell in him" (Colossians 1:19). God chose him, and God through him saves me to be alive in him. In Christ and his fullness is contained God's offer to me.

I want to reach my potential. Rob wants to reach his. You want to reach yours. But it is God who will define that potential. He will define it not on the basis of who we are but on the basis of who he is. The question is: Will you or I or any of us let God do that?

The apostle Paul focused correctly when he said, "For in Christ all the fullness of the Deity lives in bodily form" (Colossians 2:9). He is talking about Christ Jesus. In him—not us nor anything else—but in him all the fullness of God dwells in bodily form. And he goes on to say, "and you have been given fullness in Christ" (v. 10).

I am not complete because I am self-fulfilled or self-made. Neither are you. Rob's shattering experience shows us clearly that if all we had was "self-fulfillment," the self wouldn't hold up very long in our uncertain world. Rather, you and I are made complete in him. Scripture tells us that he "is the head over every power and authority. In him you were also circumcised, in the putting off of the sinful nature, not with a circumcision done by the hands of men but with the circumcision done by Christ, having been buried with him in baptism and raised with him through your faith in the power of God, who raised him from the dead" (Colossians 2:10-12).

Now on whom does that center? Not me, not you. But on him. He is the fulfillment. He is the completion for Rob, for me, for us.

God Is for Me

God is not blind to your problems or my struggles or Rob's needs. He knows all about us and stands for us, not against us. The psalmist David exclaimed: "God is for me" (Psalm 56:9). David knew it because he saw God act when he called for help. David, like us, may not have known everything, but he knew this: "God is for me." And resounding down through the ages, those words come to each of us who call on God for help: God is not against me; God is not my enemy; God is not angry with me; this I know, God is for me.

Finding Satisfaction When Life Disappoints

If I don't ever come to realize that, then I will have no larger view of life, no other way to look at what happens to me than my own perspective. Unless I see that God is for me, I will see illness, setbacks, misfortune, job loss, or broken relationships as devastating to my very life. But when I see myself from God's perspective, I see what happens to me not as barriers but bumps on a highway leading to the fulfillment God has for me.

God Isn't Deaf

You can take an exit survey some Sunday in your own church. Ask people who have had rough times in their lives why they still love God. Though you'll get various answers, you'll hear repeatedly the same theme the psalmist gives, one answer that many have made their own: "I love the LORD, for he heard my voice; he heard my cry for mercy" (Psalm 116:1).

Why do I love God? Because life is good and comfortable and easy? No. I love God because he heard me.

Sometimes marriages cool because one spouse says to the other, "You're not hearing me." Or we have trouble between parents and teenagers as one side says, "You don't listen to me." But God's ear is not deaf; he is listening. He hears us.

"I love the LORD," the psalmist said, "because he heard my voice; he heard my cry for mercy." The psalmist knew that; he experienced that. And because God listened to him before and showed his mercy before, the psalmist knew that God would listen to him again—and show mercy again. No matter how crushing life is, I can know that too. So can you, no matter how often we call to God.

In My Best Interest

The next verse reads, "Because he turned his ear to me, I will call on him as long as I live" (v. 2). "I know he hears me," the redeemed writer says. "Therefore I am going to call on him. I'm going to keep calling on him. I'm going to call on him as long as I live because God hears me." In other words, "I'm going to call and call and call." Why? Because I know he hears me.

Knowing God hears me makes me want to talk to him, to call on him. When someone offers me a listening ear, I want to talk to that person. And when that listening ear is God's ear, I find that there is a lot I want to talk with him about.

We Are Like Children

When our grandson was learning to walk, he thought he was quite free as he traveled from the kitchen to the living room, back to the dining room, and into the kitchen again. But his mother's eye was always on him. She saw where he was heading. She made sure that there wasn't anything sharp that he would fall against, and she was right there if he did fall down. When he fell, she wiped his tears; when he needed salve on a wound, she was there for him. And soon he would fall again.

I think God, who is our heavenly Father, is watching every believer in the same way—only we aren't aware of it any more than my grandson was aware of his mother. I think that is true because I hear what God says to me: "I will instruct you and teach you in the way you should go; I will counsel you and watch over you" (Psalm 32:8). As a loving parent, God wants to guide me. He watches over me carefully. I'm never beyond his watchful eye.

Finding Satisfaction When Life Disappoints

There is nothing uncertain about that. It is very clear. "I will counsel you and watch over you." I picture God watching me. I think that there have been many dangerous traps that he has kept me away from. I think that there have been many wrong turns that he has kept me from making. God shows me the way to go. He says, "I will instruct you and teach you in the way you should go."

I am like a child. Like my grandson, I think of myself as quite free and independent. But God is keeping his eye on me. I'll get along. I'll make it, unless I rebel and say, as children sometimes say, "I can walk by myself!" Then it is only a matter of time until I will fall again.

Because God Loves Me

Because God loves me, He wants to pick me up when I am down. Like you, I do fall down. And sometimes I become depressed about it. I'm not the first. Certainly the psalmist was like me. He said, "My soul faints with longing . . . my eyes fail. . . . The arrogant dig pitfalls for me. . . . men persecute me without cause. They almost wiped me from the earth" (Psalm 119:81-87). Sounds like something any of us could have said, doesn't it? "But," he continues, "I have not forsaken your precepts." And because he could say that honestly, he could go on and say, "Preserve my life according to your love" (v. 88).

The question is not, "What's happening to me?" or "What are others doing to me?" or "Why are my circumstances so bad?" or the exclamation, "How painful life is!" Rather, I need to be asking, and you need to be asking, "Am I keeping God's

In My Best Interest

precepts, his teachings, his standards?" Because if we are, then we can request, "May your unfailing love be my comfort" (Psalm 119:76). Then his lovingkindness will revive us.

Rob has found that out—not all at once, but he has found it out. "Pits dug," "soul fainting," "persecuted," "almost wiped from the earth"—he could understand. He has been there. But he has come through. God has preserved him, and he knows why. It was "according to your love."

There are still bad days. Rob is still without regular work. That's probably the way it will be from now on. His retirement income won't be what he once thought it would be. But he's moving on with new discoveries, new understanding, and a deep, deep conviction. "Your faithfulness continues" (Psalm 119:90).

Think of it! New energy to the weak—restoration, renewal, life, through God's unfailing kindness.

Where I am, what I am doing, what I face can still get me down, just as the psalmist was down at times. But always there is God's lovingkindness waiting to revive me. How can I know it's mine? Because I can say with honesty before God—with him knowing that I am telling the truth—"I have kept your precepts. I am following your Word. I am obeying you." When I can say that, and when God knows it's true, that I mean it, his lovingkindness comes to me as fresh winds of renewal and revival. He will lift me up. Have you discovered that yet?

Perspective

When at last I begin to see that God acts in my best interest, even in life's toughest times, it doesn't focus my attention inward;

When I am not in the depths of despair re failure I wonder who I KUCH. I wonder who can help to this experience @

A goal 7-15-03 1334

it focuses my attention outward. I have so much more to give to other people when I focus outward. I can live with an abandonment that is unknown to self-centered people. You can too.

And we can worship. As never before we can see our connection with God's plan and say with awe, "Thank you." Both in the difficult times and in the good times, that gives us perspective.

Isaiah is a model to us of this perspective, this right kind of thinking. He understood: "This is what the LORD says . . . 'I am the LORD your God, who teaches you what is best for you, who directs you in the way you should go'" (Isaiah 48:17). That's God's promise. But there is a warning too: "If only you had paid attention to my commands, your peace would have been like a river" (v. 18).

Easy life? He doesn't say that. No problems? No pain? He doesn't say that either. No sudden shifts in health or job or circumstances? That's not the promise. The promise to Isaiah, the promise to Israel, the promise to God's redeemed is: "I am the LORD your God" and "Your peace would have been like a river."

This is the one who loves you and me, who understands our best interests. My life has taken twists and turns; so has yours. I have hurts; so do you. But we serve the King of kings and Lord of lords. No matter what happens, no matter where we go, God is our peace. And God's peace is always there. I have learned that. Have you?

FOR REFLECTION OR DISCUSSION

1. What does it mean to you that "God doesn't want to hurt you"?

2. Why is your best interest also God's best interest?

He made me & He has a purpose for me in His greater plan. When He allows me to see that He involved me in His greater plan, I have great joy and satisfaction + hope.

In My Best Interest

3. How have you discovered that God is not deaf?

4. Knowing God has his eye on you, what difference does that make in what you are doing today?

trying to finish getting all tax info to Leo Cohean

3

I'm Worth
More Than I Thought

ONCE, FOR A FEW DAYS, we had in our home a young man who never really understood what he was worth. He tried to escape his feelings of inadequacy through illegal drugs. It didn't work. He wanted more than anything to fit in, to find his niche. But he couldn't seem to do so. In time he took the only way out that seemed to make sense to him.

He killed himself.

None of us could help him understand the possibilities for his life. He had decided he wasn't worth much.

I remember how he would pray to God. We'd get on our knees together; he would plead to God to help him. I would pray for him; others would gather around and pray for him. One night he ran the gamut from letting us lay hands on him in prayer to threatening us all with a large knife. One of the most tender memories I have is a Sunday morning when, without any urging from us, our son, then about eight years old, touched this young man's arm, looked up into his face, and said, "We are praying for you."

But the young man couldn't seem to make it. The grip of drugs was too great, the pain too overwhelming.

By contrast, one day a man telephoned me from another part of the country. "Do you know who this is?" he asked. I've never liked that kind of call; I prefer to be told right away who it is. But

I'm Worth More Than I Thought

he persisted with the "guess who" approach. No, I didn't know who he was. So he told me his name and waited. The silence on my end told him that I still wasn't making any connection. Actually, I was becoming frustrated. I did not know who the man was, nor had he yet revealed why he was calling. Finally he blurted out, "Thirty-two years ago you led me to Christ."

Slowly, as he identified the place and circumstances, bits and pieces of the scene began to come back to me. But even so, that's not where I found pleasure in the conversation. The pleasure for me was in hearing where he is now in his spiritual journey, the work he is doing as a believer, his evangelism of others, bringing them along to faith in Christ. That was the joy for me. He is spreading the flame. Not only is he multiplying what I once expended into his life, but also he is helping me to rejoice in his worth; he is helping me to rejoice in mine.

Worth Makes All the Difference

Worth—it makes all the difference in the world to us. It is the difference between life that is satisfying and fulfilled and life that has no value or meaning at all. The man who telephoned me knows what Jesus meant when he said, "I have come that they may have life, and have it to the full" (John 10:10). The other man, the one who took his own life, was never able to take hold of that offer. One has had good years, years of rewards and the joys of walking with Christ. The other lived in misery and despair. His existence seemed not only to have no meaning for him, but he was unable to see any hope for change. One man is still a celebration to others. The other man is only a memory.

Finding Satisfaction When Life Disappoints

The young man who took his own life grew up in a home warm with Christian love and teaching. His siblings to this day follow Jesus. But the other man, who is now bringing so much joy to others, didn't have that Christian heritage. Yet he met the Savior and found his worth.

I don't know how to explain what happened except that early on in his teaching, Jesus told us that there are four types of soil. No matter whether a lot of good seed is sown or only a little, the soil determines what happens. One person has a sense of worth because he finds his worth in Christ. Another doesn't.

Salvation is much more than a gateway to eternal life. It is a gateway to the discovery of our worth. I've seen that in these two men. You've seen it in people you know. I saw it in my own life. I've seen it also in the person I know best.

My wife, Andrea, spent her childhood in a home where she was always trying to please her father and stepmother. She couldn't do it. The struggles she had with her feelings of worthlessness even contributed to an asthmatic condition that kept her sick in bed. Every signal she received at home reinforced the feeling of "no worth," "no worth."

But when she was twelve years old, she was sent to another state to live with her mother. At a Bible camp nearby she heard and understood the Gospel. Then, through the nurturing of a small assembly of Christian believers, she discovered her worth—real worth—her worth to God. That changed her life. She came to be able to believe in her own worth and to love even the family that had rejected her. What happened to her touched them and many others, including me.

I'm Worth More Than I Thought

The Ripple Effect of Our Worth

We do have worth. When Ethel Waters said, "God don't make no junk," she was theologically correct. And because that is true, there is an ever-expanding influence of our worth that spreads into the lives of others. It is like a stone thrown into a pool. The ripple effect is ongoing. What starts with one person, by the investment of God, keeps on expanding.

What is one man worth? One woman? One child? God's investment knows no limits. As God works in our lives—yours and mine—an ever-expanding circle of influence spreads from us outward to others.

I am not the measure of my worth or my influence. God is. He is the one who knows the price tag I bear. He knows the price he paid to redeem me and make me his own. And he knows the investment he continues to make in me.

When God invests in me and gives me his power, and I discover my worth to him, his Word says that "greater things than this shall ye do." And it is so because as I am more and more closely attached to Christ, like the attachment of the vine and the branches, the power of multiplication from him through me increases many times over.

But, unfortunately, that doesn't happen for everyone.

One More Chance

In the story Jesus told about the seeds that fell on several different types of soil, some seeds germinated, grew, and produced; some didn't. Scripture says, "Other seed fell among

Finding Satisfaction When Life Disappoints

thorns, which grew up and choked the plants, so that they did not bear grain" (Mark 4:7). That is the other side of the story—the losing side.

No grain. All that seed sown in someone's life but no crop.

Why? Jesus explained: "But the worries of this life, the deceitfulness of wealth and the desires for other things come in and choke the word, making it unfruitful" (Mark 4:19).

Worries of the world, riches that deceive—these choke a person's spiritual life, he said. And they do. They promise so much; they give so little.

Yet I find hope in another story told by Jesus. To help us understand God's concern for us—to show his great love, Jesus weaves a picture story.

"A man had a fig tree, planted in his vineyard, and he went to look for fruit on it, but did not find any. So he said to the man who took care of the vineyard, 'For three years now I've been coming to look for fruit on this fig tree and haven't found any. Cut it down! Why should it use up the soil?'" (Luke 13:6-7).

But then came the reply: "Wait one more year. I'll give it one more chance. I've been watching with hope; I've been looking for three years. I'll give it one more chance."

And isn't that what God gives to us—one more chance? He'll work with us, encourage us. He won't easily give up on us. We are valuable to God. Jesus told that story about a fig tree, but we know whom he was really talking about. He was talking about you and me. He wants to give us another chance; he is the God of another chance—that's how much we are worth to God.

I'm Worth More Than I Thought

God Wants to Be Found Out

God is not like people who give up on us or who put us down. His investment is too great. God will work with us. He doesn't put us down because he doesn't have to.

Recently I visited a physician specialist. From the moment I entered his consulting room, he was condescending, ridiculing what I said, brushing me off in his hurry to get on to other patients who were stacked up at ten-minute appointment intervals.

I came away from that visit thinking, *Poor man. How insecure he must be. If he were certain of himself, secure in who he is as a qualified physician, he wouldn't have to behave that way. Obviously he knows he is inept. In his uncertainty he attacks—he keeps people off balance, defensive. If he was certain of his skills, he wouldn't have to fear being found out.*

God isn't like that physician. God isn't insecure; God wants to be "found out." That's why he invests in us. He doesn't have to put us down to make himself feel more able. He already is able.

As a tree in God's vineyard—planted, cultivated, looked after—it is enough to produce something faithfully. I don't have to be "great"—at least not by producing a lot. I am great on the basis of whom I obey. That gives me self-worth because I have God's definition of my worth.

God Says We Have What It Takes

I think when we get to heaven, we're going to be surprised. We're going to find people called great in heaven that we hardly noticed here, and people we think are so great here we may not

Finding Satisfaction When Life Disappoints

find in heaven at all! The great are those who do what Jesus says. Our real self-worth depends on it.

Self-worth can keep a person from crime and hate and self-destruction. The opposite is also true. Visit prisons and talk to men or women behind bars. Study their background, the shaping factors in their lives. Look at how they filtered out love and support and instead took in the negatives. Notice the insecurity that sent them chasing after acceptance. Look at the results. Each one is a person who didn't have to be that way.

You've got what it takes to be great on Jesus' terms. I've got what it takes. Some people don't want to hear that. They would rather go around saying, "I don't have what it takes." Well, if you are a Christian, you do have what it takes.

Listen to Paul's comments about that: "And God is able to make all grace abound to you, so that in all things at all times, having all that you need, you will abound in every good work" (2 Corinthians 9:8).

Can I abound in every good work? Yes, because God's grace abounds toward me. What does that mean? It means that I have been given all sufficiency to do good work. Not just partial sufficiency in some things, but all sufficiency in all things.

Now, after reading a passage like that, will I try to tell God that I don't have worth? Will you? Because God will argue with us. He says that we do!

Worth Makes a Difference

Knowing what she is worth can make the difference between a shy woman and an outgoing one who adjusts easily to life. A person who is certain of his worth has fewer adjustments to make than his friends who are still trying to discover themselves as individuals of worth. A person who still harbors feelings of uncertainty about his or her worth retreats, avoids, takes fewer chances, or, worse, takes the kind of chances that lead only to stumbling and the reinforcing of the sense of worthlessness.

I know a person who is gifted, talented, intelligent, attractive. She has it all. But she doesn't know that. So she is always putting down others. It is almost as though by pointing out the weaknesses or failures of others, she thinks she gains stature. It's a bit like racism—if you can knock down others, you will feel more important yourself. Do you know people who do that? God doesn't want us to live that way.

God cares very much how each of us is developing, how we are growing. We want God to be at work in us. We pray for him to be at work in us. We let God do what he wants to do. Then we are secure enough to let God do his work in someone else too.

Breaking Out of the Darkness

When someone I love very much learned that his wife no longer wanted to stay married to him, he went into overwhelming depression. It was a battle to hold steady while shame and guilt and hopelessness washed over him. It was a turn in life he never expected.

We all know that life can take some of those tough turns. We go from bright sunshine into deep darkness, and we wonder how we are going to get through it. The dark seems to be all

Finding Satisfaction When Life Disappoints

around; we can't see. When it happens to one close to me, and it has, I agonize with that loved one. It hurts so much. And though I can only watch from the sidelines as I see pain sweep over that loved one, and though I try to reassure and put my arms around that person as we cry together, helplessness still descends.

I have to go beyond myself and try to help that person go beyond himself. There is only one who can quiet the pain-wracked spirit, only one who can restore and heal, only one who can rebuild and give back the feelings of worth that have been ripped away. God is the only one who can.

In the hurting times like that, I turn to Psalm 112:4: "Even in darkness light dawns for the upright." The darkness is there; it is real, but it doesn't last. Light does come. It's God's light. God is light and God is there. Darkness will not stay forever. God can and does bring us out.

The psalmist is right: "Even in darkness light dawns. . . ." And light will come for you. When a person's heart is breaking, that pain is deep, that wound is real. It's not something that can be corrected in a moment or with a quick treatment. It takes time. It takes care. It takes love before healing begins. God knows that. That hurt does not lessen your worth to God any more than your child is worth less to you when she comes home crying with skinned knees.

God understands your broken heart. You are precious to him. Don't run away from God. The best thing you can do is stop, turn, be quiet, and let him heal your broken heart and bind up your wounds. You will know when he's doing it. And as he does it, you will sense how much you are loved. You will see once again how much you are worth.

I'm Worth More Than I Thought

A Focused Mind

My two friends, the one who killed himself and the one who went on to a life of faithfulness and satisfaction, are a microcosm of our world. People everywhere fit into both categories, and millions are in between. Our worth, though clear to God, is only clear to us as we let God show us. And when he does, our worth is only as real to us as our willingness to say, "O Lord, you have given me worth, and I accept the worth you have placed in me."

We are an anxious people; we don't always live out our worth. So many of our uncertainties and much of our ongoing inner confusion come from not letting God bring out in us the worth he places there.

The apostle Paul, understanding the conflict between our anxieties and the awareness of our worth, was so graphic. He used picture language to talk about the conflict that you and I feel. It is pretty hard to miss what he is saying. "The mind of sinful man is death, but the mind controlled by the Spirit is life and peace" (Romans 8:6).

Why then am I so anxious? Why are you? The spiritually controlled mind is life and peace. It is life because God is alive, and he has taken up residence in us. He is from everlasting to everlasting, and the life he has given us is everlasting too. The spiritually controlled mind is peace because God is peace. Peace is an everlasting quality of God, and God gives us his peace.

Our lack of peace comes from focusing on turmoil, on what is failing and collapsing and being destroyed. Peace that stays comes from focusing on what is whole and can't be taken away or destroyed. What did Jesus say? "Peace I leave with you; my

Finding Satisfaction When Life Disappoints

peace I give you. I do not give to you as the world gives. Do not let your hearts be troubled and do not be afraid" (John 14:27).

Where is your mind focused? When I get up in the morning and pick up my Bible for my morning devotions, I read about what God gives—life, health, peace, joy, and so much more. Then I say, "Today, no matter what comes, that is what I will focus on." That is the proof of my worth.

I can do that because at last I am coming to understand that God's peace is always there. And it is there for me. Have you discovered that God's peace is there for you?

FOR REFLECTION OR DISCUSSION

1. How do you measure your true worth?

2. Can you think of a time when God has given you a second chance?

3. What does "all sufficiency" mean specifically to you, where you are right now?

4. What hope does the psalmist see for those who are going through a "dark valley"? (Psalm 112:4). Have you proved this verse true in your own experience? If you are in that valley, what is your part in coming through it?

4

PEACE IS
ALWAYS THERE

ONE EVENING ON THE DRIVE home from my office, I was listening to National Public Radio. The announcer was interviewing teenagers who wanted to commit suicide—slow suicide. One boy explained, "I got a needle from this guy I know who has AIDS and injected his blood into me. I feel so free now. I don't have to think about anything anymore. I feel so free." He thought he had found a way to peace. I don't think he did.

If you were to go to one of the larger boat shows in the United States, you would find acres of boats—some small, mostly large. Some yachts are worth more than a million dollars. You might be approached by a handsome, personable salesman with a winning smile and a deep, resonant voice. He would explain to you the features and delights you would have in owning an expensive boat. What you wouldn't know is that the salesman only a few years ago was the senior minister of a very large prestigious church. But he left his church, and he left his family. This minister-turned-salesman has redefined his lifestyle, and his life no longer includes God. He may think he has found peace. I don't think he has.

During World War II, when John Paul Sartre wrote his book *Being and Nothingness*, he was a member of the French Resistance. He felt that life is absurd, that there is no God. So he taught that

Peace Is Always There

we create our own idea of God in order to give meaning to our lives. It's each person's way to find peace, Sartre thought. Out of his teaching came existentialism, a philosophy holding that *we* alone determine right from wrong. We form our own direction as best we can. That, to Sartre, was the only way to have peace. I don't think he found it, but his teaching has influenced millions.

God Is Peace and God Is Always There

Everywhere there are voices telling us how we can find peace. People want peace, but so many never find what they're looking for.

I meet people who don't have peace. They look for it through pleasure-seeking, therapy, new sexual relationships, alcohol, drugs. They are unhappy; they have pain, but they try to deal with it the best way they know how. Often I find myself praying for them, asking God to help them to know what millions of people do know—real peace, the peace of God. That peace is not just the result of the end of wars or fighting within ourselves or with others. It is a complete peace, a perfect peace, because it is God's peace.

People look everywhere searching for that kind of deep inner peace when all the time peace is right there. God is peace, and God is always there.

Isaiah the prophet explained the way to peace: "You will keep in perfect peace him whose mind is steadfast, because he trusts in you" (Isaiah 26:3). God does the keeping. It's his peace—perfect peace. That's what so many people are longing for.

"You will *keep* in perfect peace." That means fixed. That

Finding Satisfaction When Life Disappoints

means locked in place. God offers us a perfect peace that is locked in place.

For many years *Decision* magazine had a consulting editor in Canada by the name of Les Tarr. He was also the editor of *Faith Today* magazine. Les is in heaven now, but for more than twenty-five years he was paralyzed. Sometimes he had to spend weeks in the hospital. Pain was always his companion.

Les started out as a pastor in the central part of Canada. But he became ill, then paralyzed. He could have looked at his circumstances and said, "My career is gone. No more opportunities. Nothing ahead for me." But he looked to God's promises—something deeper and greater than his immediate circumstances. As a result, Les had God's peace.

He became a writer, and a good one. He wrote for *Christianity Today* and the *Toronto Star*, and he taught at Ontario Bible College. He also wrote a little publication called *Have a Good Day*. Yet Les was always in pain—excruciating pain. I used to tell discouraged writers, "Do you know that the man who writes *Have a Good Day* hasn't had a good day himself in twenty-five years?"

Les had to leave the pulpit where he may have ministered to hundreds. God opened the door for him to write, and he ministered to millions. I knew him. He was a man who had peace.

I'm So Useless!

Failing health? What an opportunity for God's peace. Difficulties? What an opportunity for God's peace. But people say to me, "I feel so useless. How can I have peace when I feel this way?" Someone else once said that, someone familiar to many Christians.

Charlotte Elliot felt useless. But that "uselessness" is what God used; and because God did, millions of people for generations have been touched by her music. God made more of something less—and in the process gave peace.

Charlotte Elliot had a plain, unexciting life. She was thirty-three years old, unmarried, and in those days (1822) life for an unmarried woman did not mean a successful career; it meant staying home in her father's house. That's what she did. Her father was a vicar near London. When she was thirty-two, she suffered a severe illness that left her an invalid for the remaining fifty years of her life.

In 1834 she went to live with her brother, the minister at St. Mary's Anglican Church in Brighton. There was one event she was looking forward to in her otherwise drab life—one event. The church was sponsoring a bazaar to raise money to educate the daughters of needy clergy. But just before the event she became so ill she couldn't attend.

She looked at her frail health, her apparent uselessness, and began to be overwhelmed by spiritual doubts. She kept saying, "I am so useless. So useless." Other people even commented about her worries, the spiritual conflict. "I'm not good for anything. I'm so useless." Peace? She had anything but peace.

Yet, alone, while the rest of the family was at that church bazaar, as Charlotte Elliot struggled with those emotions and doubts about her own salvation, she realized that her comfort was not in her feelings or in the events or circumstances of her life, but in what Christ had done for her. That's when this

Finding Satisfaction When Life Disappoints

invalid, this sickly woman who thought she was so useless, wrote that hymn, "Just As I Am, Without One Plea."

Within a decade that hymn was being sung everywhere. D. L. Moody, the great evangelist, said that hymn touched more hearts and brought more people to Christ than any other hymn written. And for nearly twenty-five years I watched people respond by the thousands as that song was sung at the Billy Graham Crusades.

Charlotte Elliot died fifty years after she became an invalid, and in her possession were found more than 1,000 letters from people who were helped by that hymn. People who, because of her trust, found Christ. People who, from her peace, also found peace.

One song! It came out of her despondency; it came out of her doubt; it came out of her feelings of worthlessness and useless-ness. Yet we can hear the surrender in her words, "Just as I am, without one plea/But that Thy blood was shed for me/And that Thou bid'st me come to Thee,/O Lamb of God, I come! I come!"

Then that second part—can you hear it? Charlotte Elliot was saying, "Just as I am, poor, wretched, blind/Sight, riches, heal-ing of the mind,/Yea, all I need in Thee to find—/O Lamb of God, I come! I come!"

God Is Not Far Away

What circumstance, what situation has you down? God isn't absent. God isn't far away. God is close. Are you in pain? Are you alone? Are you ill? May I say it kindly: What an opportu-nity for God to give you his peace.

Peace Is Always There

my inadequacy

✗   Where is your focus? Where is it even now? Can you focus on Christ who gives peace? Can you do it not to escape your pain but to let God meet you in the midst of your pain?

One Sunday I was preaching in a church in Sacramento, California. During the message I told the story of a woman I had met in Pittsburgh, Pennsylvania, where she was counseling at a Billy Graham Crusade.

That woman told me: "I have two sons; both of them are in prison. But God has taken that pain, and He has shown me that those boys have made their own choices; they'll have to answer to God for what they've done, not to me." She said, "At first, I thought I could not counsel at this crusade. How could I counsel others when my own sons are in prison? But I find that God is leading me to women like me whose children are like mine, and I have a ministry." She was a woman at peace.

At the end of the service in which I told the woman's story, a couple came to me and said, "We don't go to this church. We're visiting here today from Seattle, Washington. When you told that story about the woman whose two sons are in prison, that story touched us." Then the woman said, "Our son is in prison. He murdered his wife and his three children."

I put my arms around both of them. I could feel their pain as I prayed for them and asked for God's peace to surround them. I prayed for their son. I prayed because I knew that every waking moment their minds would go back to asking: "What could we have done? Are we to blame?"

Then the father told me, "You know why your illustration about the woman counseling helped us? Because we were on a short-term mission trip in Papua New Guinea when we learned

Finding Satisfaction When Life Disappoints

what our son had done. When we came home, we weren't sure if we could ever do missionary work again. But we can!" They had found God's deeper peace.

Now why is that story so important to each of us? Because none of us is immune to tragedy. All around us are people in need, as we are in need. For many, their world is in pieces—but we have for ourselves and for others the Gospel of peace.

During the Long and Dark Nights

This week someone will be told he has lost his job; we can offer him God's peace.

This week someone will learn she has cancer; we can pray for God's peace.

This week two people will discover that their marriage is in trouble; we can ask God to surround that couple with his peace.

This week someone will start to slide into depression; God offers his peace.

Many will wonder, "Can I go on?" We bring to them the Gospel of peace. To a world in pieces, we are bringers of peace. And with God's peace, we are given a way to endure.

A man I have learned to admire, who has helped me so much with my understanding of Scripture and with guidance in preaching, is the man who was once called "the prince of preachers." His name? Charles Haddon Spurgeon. I suppose I turn to his commentaries more than any others when I have an opportunity to preach. He's an inspiration to me. Yet famous preacher that he was, Charles Haddon Spurgeon had his private pain. For forty years, all of London talked of his messages. His sermons were even printed in U.S. newspapers; the world knew him. But not many knew that he had such inner turmoil, such long periods of dark, deep depression that sometimes he had to go away for an extended time to recover.

Would I want that in my life? Would you? And yet it was that pain, that depression that gave such depth to this man—not only to his preaching, but to those commentaries that people still use today. And who would have wanted to have the burden of Mrs. Spurgeon? How many long nights must she have spent praying for her husband, wondering if he would come out of the darkness, each time wondering if his depression would ever end.

Well, God loved Charles Haddon Spurgeon and used him and brought peace to this man over and over again. Spurgeon endured, even when he seemed to have lost God's peace. God kept bringing peace back to him. God will do the same for you and for me.

We Couldn't Do It if We Didn't Know

Scripture meets us with the help we need. The same Scripture that says, "Keep your head in all situations," goes on to tell us to "endure hardship."

Endure. What does that mean? It means to continue in the same state. It means to remain firm under suffering. It means to hold steady. It means, don't yield.

That's hard to do, and we couldn't do it, and we couldn't help others do it if we didn't know that "He alone is my rock and my salvation," as the psalmist tells us (Psalm 62:2).

Finding Satisfaction When Life Disappoints

We couldn't do it if we didn't know that "you have . . . delivered my feet from stumbling" (Psalm 56:13).

We couldn't do it if we weren't certain: "'For I know the plans I have for you,' declares the LORD, 'plans to prosper you and not to harm you, plans to give you hope and a future,'" as the prophet Jeremiah told us (Jeremiah 29:11).

We could not do it if we did not know our Lord was telling the truth when he said, "I am with you always, to the very end of the age" (Matthew 28:20).

We could not make it if we did not believe with all our hearts the Master's words: "Peace I leave with you; my peace I give you. I do not give to you as the world gives. Do not let your hearts be troubled and do not be afraid" (John 14:27).

Jesus offers his peace to each of us. I can slap it away, of course. I don't have to take it. I've seen people do that, and I've seen the results in their lives. Some push away the peace that Jesus offers because they have convinced themselves that they shouldn't have it. They're abused and they're hurting. "Peace isn't for me," they say. "I don't have peace; I can't have peace. Life has brought too many hurts."

I have heard it; you have heard it; we have all talked with people who say it. They decide that God has no interest in them.

They are wrong, of course. Very wrong.

And when we read the Scriptures, we see how wrong they are. We see how much God does care about them.

God says, "'I have seen his ways, but I will heal him; I will guide him and restore comfort to him, creating praise on the lips of the mourners in Israel. Peace, peace to those far and near,' says the LORD. 'And I will heal them'" (Isaiah 57:18-19).

"I have seen, but I will heal," he says.

"I know," says God, "but I will restore."

Maybe a person has done something he thinks has ruined his life. "I will heal," God says. "Peace to those far and near."

That's the power and the wonder of what God does. "I will heal," he says.

That's what God longs to do for anyone if he or she will let him. Think of it. Peace at last. Healing of our brokenness at last. "I will guide him and restore comfort to him." Think of that. What a wonderful promise that is.

Would I Really Want That?

Let me tell another story. This too is about the writer of a hymn—Joseph Scriven. Because I write, I have sometimes found myself saying, "Oh, if only I could pen such words as 'What a friend we have in Jesus/All our sins and griefs to bear!'"

But then I can hear Jesus saying to me, "Roger, would you really have wanted to have written those words in a situation like his?"

Joseph Scriven wrote that hymn recovering from terrible heartache. He was about to be married. *This wonderful woman is going to marry me!* It was all he could think about. *Tomorrow is our wedding day—joy of joys! Tomorrow I will be wed.* But that night, hours before the wedding, she drowned. That's when he wrote the poem "What a Friend We Have in Jesus." He put it away. He didn't publish it then—not yet.

Years later he moved to Canada to live near Rice Lake, Ontario, where he earned his living tutoring children. Nearly twenty years passed, and, wonder of wonders, he fell in love again. God had provided another. Once more he was planning for that happy day. *At last I'll have a partner in this life!* But shortly before the wedding, his fiancée died of pneumonia. And that poem, kept so long in a bottom drawer, was set to music, "What a Friend We Have in Jesus."

Joseph Scriven spent the rest of his days alone. Yet he was known by the people around him as a consistent Christian. What a wonderful title: "consistent Christian." A man who had something deeper than what most people had, a personal close Friend. And he had what that Friend gave him. He had peace.

When Scriven died, the premier of his province, E. C. Drury, said, "He did not build a railroad or amass a fortune; he contributed a thought—one thought—a thought that will outlive railroads and fortunes."

One thought. That's what Scriven published, and it has blessed millions. Would I like to bless millions with just one thought? Would I have liked to be that man? I can hear our Lord saying, "I loved him, and I was his All in all; I filled his need for love, and I gave him my peace.

"I love you, too," he says to you and me. "I'll fill your needs too. I'll give you my peace."

Promises to Cling To

How is God going to meet me in the years ahead? How is God going to meet you? What is God going to do with you this year or next as he gives you that peace—the kind that passes all understanding?

Peace Is Always There

Here are a couple of promises for us to cling to. Even a branch that is broken can be bound up. It can bear fruit again. Even a candle that has just a spark left in it can blaze again and can light hundreds, even thousands, of other candles. It's never too late to receive peace. Not with God it isn't.

That promise is there for us in Scripture where it says, "A bruised reed he will not break, and a smoldering wick he will not snuff out" (Isaiah 42:3). Your little flame, your flickering oil lamp, your stub of a candle, your clouded lantern may be about out, but it isn't out yet. And God won't extinguish it. Even a broken life isn't destroyed yet. None of us is beyond fanning into bright flame. God's promise brings life. His promise offers wholeness, healing. His promise is for peace. God won't extinguish a dimly burning wick. God won't break the bruised reed.

We bruised reeds know who we are. We who are smoldering wicks know we are hardly lighted. We know what hopelessness feels like. But we are never without hope, according to the promise of God.

Claim Isaiah 42:3. Don't give up, because God isn't giving up on you.

Peace for Me? Yes!

Will I always be searching for peace? No!

Will I always be tossed around by my own impressions, the attitudes of other people, the changes in the culture? No!

If peace is always there, can I find and keep that peace? Yes!

Around us other people may use that word *peace*, but we know that many really don't understand it. We hear talk of

Finding Satisfaction When Life Disappoints

international peace, national peace, peace among races and cultures, individual peace in the midst of tribulation and confusion and uncertainty; and many of us wonder, *So few seem to have it or even know what it is—can peace really be for me?* Yes, it can.

When Jesus gave his promise of peace, it was a confusing time for the disciples and for the world. But he said it then and he says it now: "In me you may have peace" (John 16:33).

It isn't going to come from anywhere else or anyone else. That peace is only in Christ. I've seen that peace discovered by people who have a terminal illness. I've seen it come to people who have lost their families or their jobs. I've seen it in people whose personal world has collapsed. "In me," Jesus said, "you may have peace."

He went on, "In this world you will have trouble." He was right about that. We do. And he probably won't take us out of it. We are in this world. We will face tough times. You may be facing a terribly tough time right now. But listen to Jesus again: "But take heart! I have overcome the world." The world that's giving you and me such trouble is the world that he has already overcome. He's the ultimate victor. "Take heart." He said it then and he says it now. The world will tell you to find peace within yourself. But Jesus said, "I have overcome the world." That's good news.

God's peace doesn't come from outward circumstances. God's peace is inside. It doesn't go away, no matter what is happening outside. That's real peace. Jesus Christ gives that peace.

Concentrate on his gift. The world may be full of trouble, and the people in it may be troublemakers; there may not be peace anywhere else. But the ones who trust in Christ, who are united with him, have real peace—deep peace. The peace of God. "My peace," he said.

Think about that—"my peace"; that's what he is offering you.

With that peace you no longer have to have a troubled heart. You no longer have to be afraid. You no longer have to be discouraged. You no longer have to feel as though you are a failure. That is not what Jesus wants. He wants you to be at peace.

"Over Here, with Me"

Remember what Jesus did for the disciples when they needed help? One day they were discouraged. You can read about it in John 21. You've been discouraged like they were. I've been discouraged like that.

I'll set the scene for you. Simon Peter, Thomas, Nathaniel, John, and at least two others had gone fishing. They were professionals; they knew what they were doing. They worked hard all night fishing, but they didn't catch anything. They tried, oh, they tried; no one could ever say they didn't. They all knew what to do, yet nothing happened.

You've done that. You've worked hard. You've done your best. You've done everything you know to do, and nothing has happened.

All night they worked. Then, in the morning Jesus called to them from the shore, "Friends, haven't you any fish?" (v. 5).

And they had to answer, "No."

He went right to the heart of their discouragement. "You haven't accomplished much, have you?"

Finding Satisfaction When Life Disappoints

They had to answer, "No."

Then Jesus told them what to do, and they hauled in all those fish—what a catch!

Jesus didn't stop there. He never does. He said, "Bring some of the fish you have just caught" (v. 10). And Jesus already had fish cooking, along with some bread. They not only had success, but he gave them more. Our Lord does that for us. "Come over here," he said, "and eat with me." No rebuke. No lecture. No putting them down. What love! "Come over here and eat with me."

That's the loving Savior we serve. And it was in that setting, when they were with Jesus, that he said those words that we need to hear when we need his peace so much: "Follow me" (v. 19).

Because it was in that setting, Peter began to ask questions about John: "Lord, what about him?" (v. 21).

Jesus told him not to worry about other people. "If I want him to remain alive until I return, what is that to you? You must follow me" (v. 22).

"Follow me! If I want John to be exiled in old age on the Isle of Patmos and write letters that will bless and influence the church for centuries to come, what is that to you? Follow me."

I think Jesus answers our questions about other people and their seeming (to us) successes and their apparent good fortune, or their position that seems better than our own, in the same way: "What is that to you? Follow me!" What a doorway to peace in those words: "Follow me."

Sometimes the greatest peace does not come from being successful; rather, it's in that time on the shore by the fire that we spend with our Lord Jesus Christ. He invites us into that special relationship with himself. There he feeds us and nurtures us and

59

encourages us and blesses us and gives us a whole new challenge, a commission. And, above all, he gives us his peace.

Then Jesus sends us out in his strength and love and peace, just as he sent out the disciples. Because I am really a spiritual me, he says to me what he said to them: "I know what life holds for you. I know what tomorrow holds for you. I'll give you my peace. Follow me."

FOR REFLECTION OR DISCUSSION

1. Are you feeling useless? What does God say about that? *8-4-03*
2. Where is your focus right now? *paying for the nursery*
3. How are you treating God's promise: "I will heal; I will restore"?

4. Are you opening yourself to the offer of Jesus: "In me you may have peace" (John 16:33)? If not, what steps can you take to do so? *Started this chapter randomly @ P957 – will read the whole chapters.*

5

BECAUSE I'M
REALLY A SPIRITUAL ME

IT IS TIME TO return to my story.

Would my family ever come to faith? During my early years as a believer, I began to doubt it. For me, spiritually, it was a low point, even though I'd had that encounter with God in the library of Wayne State University, an encounter that gave me real peace about my own salvation. I knew God was real. Yet without experience with the ways of God, without biblical resources to draw on (I had no Bible teaching or Sunday school training before becoming a Christian), I began to think that there was no hope for my family. For two years I had prayed for them. I began to believe that God couldn't reach my family. And that's what I told my praying friends.

But those praying friends were not like me. They did have experiences with God's faithfulness, and they did know God's Word. They prayed for me, and they prayed for my family. And one day a friend gave me a verse to hang onto: "If we believe not, yet he abideth faithful: he cannot deny himself" (2 Timothy 2:13 KJV).

That message from God went right to the core of my being. I clung to it. God isn't limited by my limited faith. God is going to be faithful to who he is in himself and to what he says. God still loved the world, and that included those I loved, too.

Because I'm Really a Spiritual Me

My Lack of Faith Didn't Limit God

In the months that followed, one by one, my family did come to faith in Christ. This is how it happened.

My brother Nelson, who is two years older than I, had a high school friend who was a Christian. Occasionally they had even gone to Sunday school together some years before. A seed had been planted. Nelson remembers that he began to go to church with me, and we would talk about my decision for Christ. One day in the car we talked seriously about Christ. I asked him if there was any reason why he could not accept Christ as his personal Savior, and he said no, there really wasn't.

That day Nelson prayed, asking Christ into his heart. It was a day of rejoicing for me. I had more than a brother. Now I had a brother in Christ. God was working. My earlier lack of faith had not limited God.

My sister Gail picks up the sequence. "I was about fourteen years old. You had already accepted the Lord, and the family kind of rejected you at that time, especially Mom and Dad. They picked on you. They were very much against it all.

"I remember thinking that you had changed because you used to fly off the handle in a moment. Someone could just look at you cross-eyed and you'd get angry; I remember that. But you didn't become angry anymore. I would deliberately try to bait you and make you angry; I wanted to say something that would bring out the old Roger. But you would not respond in the way that you had before. I asked you why, and you told me, 'Because Jesus has made a difference in my life, and I don't respond like I used to.' I remember thinking, *Hmm. I wonder how long that will*

Finding Satisfaction When Life Disappoints

last. But it did last. I could see a change in your personality and definitely in your temper, because before it really didn't take anything to get you going.

"But then Nelson started going to church, and it wasn't long before he too accepted the Lord. So there were two in the family. And that left Dad, Mother, and myself."

Gail goes on to explain what happened, including something that I said to her that embarrasses me now for its immature zeal, but God chose to use it in her life anyway. Gail said, "One night Mom became very ill. She was hemorrhaging, and they took her to the hospital by ambulance. Dad went with her, of course, and they told him that she had a blood count of zero, and they didn't know if she would make it to morning.

"I said, 'We need to pray.' And you said, 'But God will not hear you, Gail, because you don't know him.' So I said, 'Well, you pray.' And you prayed, and I prayed with you. I remember your prayer was for her health, getting her through this terrible night. My prayer was, 'If you bring Mother through this, then I will go to church, or at least consider you.' Dad called later, or early in the morning, to say that she'd had blood transfusions and was doing much better. She was going to be fine, but it would take some time.

"But your words hit me so hard. It really was what you said: 'God will not hear you because you don't belong to him.' Afterwards I thought, *He's right; God can't hear me. I don't belong to him. How can I expect God to hear me?* I remember where we were; we were in the living room. I can picture where the chairs were; it was that dramatic to me. It was really your words that got me going."

Because I'm Really a Spiritual Me

Years later, as we talked about this, I said, "I can't believe I told you God couldn't hear you." Gail replied, "Even though you don't think that was the most appropriate thing to say, it got me thinking. God couldn't hear me because I didn't belong to him. I was not his child. I remember thinking, *I want to go to church. I will at least go with an open mind.* You see, organ music turned me off. It made me ill. But I was willing to go to church."

Something So Spectacular

That night when my mother was taken to the hospital and Gail and I prayed, God did something so spectacular that it can only be explained as a miracle of God. Here's what happened. We had as the leader of our college-age youth group a church member who was a surgeon. He knew my longings; he prayed often for my family.

The night when my mother went to the hospital, this surgeon friend was home in bed asleep. His phone rang. It was the hospital summoning him to emergency surgery. He told me later that he did what he always did. Before even getting dressed, he knelt by his bed and prayed for the patient he would operate on. It wasn't until he reached the hospital that he discovered who his patient was—my mother. In the city of Detroit, with two and a half million residents, God had placed the right surgeon with the right patient. God used that doctor to save my mother's life.

Some weeks later, as my mother sat in his office in a postoperative visit, the doctor shut the door and spoke directly and

Finding Satisfaction When Life Disappoints

clearly to her about her need for the Savior. In her eighties, Mom still remembered what he told her that day: "With God's help, I was able to save your life, because you were an hour away from a coma and three hours away from death." There, in the doctor's office, my mother prayed to invite Christ into her heart as her Savior and Lord.

Gail continues, "I had come to a point where I knew I really did want to accept Jesus as my personal Savior. That Sunday, after Mom's prayer in the doctor's office, all three of us went forward in church at the invitation to accept Christ. The whole church was in tears because they had been praying for us for a long time. Dad was crying the hardest. For Dad, that first step into the aisle was so moving, the reality of it all. He cried all the way up there, and I remember him standing there with tears rolling down his face. It's one of my favorite memories."

When my parents and sister were baptized on March 31, 1957, I knew that God had done something greater than I could ask or think. What was hopeless to me ("Some people will never believe," I'd said) was not hopeless to God. My mother later explained, "It seems as if God had to bring us to our senses."

When God Changes a Person

Forty years later, in her eighties, my mother remembered my conversion and my church attendance as something that she encouraged. But back then I knew I was alone and rejected. I can still feel that hurt. No one who has felt that kind of rejection can ever deny those feelings. But God used that pain because he was able to show me: "Look, I am not limited by your weak faith.

Your doubts don't control me." And over the years as a pastor, a campus chaplain, a magazine editor, I've been able to say to so many who feel the pain of hopelessness, "God isn't limited. I know he isn't. God does bring about his miracles in his time."

My mother went on to become a Sunday school teacher to children, and a good one. She did it for many years. The children are all grown now, but many recall the influence she had on their lives and thanked her.

As for my dad, well, we need to see how much God changes a person. When I was still in my spiritual doubts, yet longing for my family, I encouraged evangelistic callers from the church to visit my parents. They were not welcome. Dad would become angry and burst out with, "Why don't they mind their own business. If I want God, I'll find God. I don't need these people . . ."

But that all changed the day he wept and received Christ into his heart. Soon Dad became one of those church evangelistic callers. He wanted others to find what he had found. The day came when he even headed the church evangelistic callers. And later, when my parents moved and began attending another church, Dad established a team of evangelistic callers in that church too.

God once asked, "Is anything too hard for the LORD?" (Genesis 18:14), and the answer has to be, "No, there isn't." Nothing I face in my life and nothing you face in yours is too hard for the Lord. Early on, as a young believer, God showed that to me in the work he did with my family. And today that work of God goes on, spreading out through my sister's children, my brother's children, and our children. All have con-

Finding Satisfaction When Life Disappoints

fessed the Savior and are passing along to their own children the faith that became real to my parents through the miraculous work of God so many years before.

The Longings Are There

Each of us has spiritual longings. I had them long before I came to saving faith. Before she died my mother told me that she had those spiritual longings too, as did my dad. God gives those longings. They may be pushed down, even denied and fought against for years. But they are there.

God has placed that longing in each person. Saint Augustine was right when he said, "You have made us for yourself, and our hearts are restless until they rest in you." When we finally come to an end of ourselves, when we stop fighting God, all that God intended for us begins to come true.

In my family, each one recognized a longing, an awareness that there has to be "more to me than what I am seeing now." That spiritual longing is there in every person.

Certainly inside each of us there is much more than others see. We are spiritual persons; God made us with a need for him to fill our lives. But the journey to discovering that too often sends us off in different directions, searching here, searching there.

I have friends—seniors, Boomers, generation Xers—and they are taking different roads in their quest for spiritual meaning. They are alike in their need, even while behaving differently in their search for answers to that need. Age, environment, the political and social systems—all become windows through

Because I'm Really a Spiritual Me

which we see the world and our own spiritual lives. Those windows we look through face in different directions.

I've met people who won't listen to their own hearts or the pleas of others urging them to receive spiritual wholeness. They listen to the Devil's lie that they are complete in themselves. Some go all the way to their death and on into an eternity apart from God, telling themselves they are right. They listen to no one else. I've also met a lot of people who, although they do listen, still don't understand.

Jesus encountered both types. One time when he was teaching a crowd, he began his teaching with these words: "Listen to me, everyone, and understand" (Mark 7:14). Jesus wanted a twofold response—listen and understand. He still does.

Some won't even listen. If the words come from Jesus, they aren't interested. Others do listen. Sometimes they even like the teaching, but they don't understand. When Jesus teaches, they filter what he says through their own experience. They hear themselves, yet they call it listening to Jesus. That is happening to people around us. We are living in an eclectic time, a cafeteria age of wanting God but wanting God on our own terms, served up the way we want our religion served. We live in a spiritual time with people wanting to make God in their own image. They don't deny that they are spiritual people. But they try to fill that spiritual need their own way. They end up with a god no bigger than themselves.

Is there a more significant spiritual answer than the cafeteria of options that makes me choose this or that to believe in on different days at different times? The answer, of course, is yes!

Finding Satisfaction When Life Disappoints

God Isn't Like Me

If God were as changeable as I am, I would always be seeking a new god on my current terms. But God isn't like me. God doesn't change. We come to him on his terms; he doesn't come to us on ours. I can meet God, but when I do, I quickly see that God is bigger than my grasp of him. Listen and understand, Jesus said. It takes both. People who listen to Jesus and understand what he is saying find what they are searching for. People who listen and understand do at last know who God is and they know who they are.

The person who comes to Jesus needs to hear and understand. The Gospel will be rejected so long as those whose minds are already made up root their convictions in their own wants, their own understanding, their own personal drive for satisfaction. They focus on themselves, trying to fill the spiritual longing that God placed in them, and they miss God.

They aren't consistent about their spirituality either. People who stand for their own spirituality but against Jesus are often emotional about their beliefs. But they are rarely consistent in their logic. That's not new; it has always been that way.

When Jesus was on trial, Scripture says, "Many were giving false testimony against Him, and yet their testimony was not consistent" (Mark 14:56 NASB). Not consistent! That's a mark of the person who wants to be the source of his own spiritual answers. He isn't logical. His emotions will take him in many directions, even contradictory ones. Until a person will admit that what Jesus said is true: "No one can come to me unless the Father who sent me draws him" (John 6:44), he or she will not find the spiritual answers God wants that person to have.

Because I'm Really a Spiritual Me

Rather, he will be his own spiritual guide with only his own beliefs. Logic comes from the transformed mind, and the transformed mind comes from the mind of Christ in us.

Am I Inconsistent Too?

But before I appear to be too harsh with others, I have to ask myself: Is my own spiritual obedience and conviction consistent? I have to ask that because I can easily substitute my own faith weaknesses for the faith strengths that God has for me.

Peter was inconsistent. Am I like Peter? Peter gave a strongly worded false witness when he denied Jesus. Then he did it again later on when other apostles had to challenge him because he was inconsistent in his behavior.

The first time Peter was inconsistent was because he just hadn't given enough thought to his own weaknesses. He did not know that followers of Jesus can never get too comfortable with their commitment to Christ. Commitment can change.

Peter spent three years with Jesus. When his trial was approaching, Jesus warned the disciples of the danger of falling away. Remember the words of Peter? He said emphatically—not me! He said, "'Even if all fall away, I will not'" (Mark 14:29). But he did.

The second time Peter was inconsistent was when he was trying to live by a double standard. He was one way with the Gentiles when his Jewish brothers weren't around, but the opposite when his Jewish brothers showed up. The apostle Paul said, "I opposed him to his face, because he was clearly in the wrong" (Galatians 2:11). As a result of being inconsistent, Peter confused

Finding Satisfaction When Life Disappoints

others too. "The other Jews joined him in his hypocrisy, so that by their hypocrisy even Barnabas was led astray" (Galatians 2:13).

It is easy to slip, to become so confident in our own relationship to Christ that we are not alert to our inconsistencies. Then we may lead others astray just as Peter was beginning to do. Fortunately for Peter, Paul challenged him. I need people to challenge me. You do too.

I expect inconsistency from those who oppose the Savior. They have religious beliefs that are very real to them, but these are not based on the Rock, Christ Jesus. When they stand against Jesus, our challenge may show just how inconsistent they are. But if we then act as Peter acted, even though we claim the name "Christian," we are inconsistent in our witness too. People will say, "See, they are not consistent either," and never be forced to look at their own inconsistencies—only at ours. They will be satisfied in their self-faith. Inconsistency was condemned in believers back then. Inconsistency still is.

I am inconsistent as well when I deny the soul-needs of people by teaching that right moral behavior, right government policies, the practice of Christian virtues will make people behave as Christians. Even if I could convince everyone in this land to think like me, behave like me, vote like me, would they then be Christians?

No "Ism" Saves

Religious liberalism doesn't save. Religious conservatism doesn't save. No "ism" saves; Jesus saves. Scripture is true: "Salvation is found in no one else, for there is no other name

Because I'm Really a Spiritual Me

under heaven given to men by which we must be saved" (Acts 4:12). No "ism" will substitute. One of my Canadian friends liked to say, "Every 'ism' soon becomes a 'wasm.'"

It was Samuel Moffett, the great missionary statesman, who said to Christians, "Christ should define our mission. Anything more is idolatry, and anything less is no longer Christian. Only God can build a Kingdom whose promised King is Jesus Christ, Lord of Life."[1]

In 1984 Bob Gudzwaard published *Idols of Our Time.* He said, "We know from Scripture that both persons and societies can put their faith in things or forces which their own hands have made. But gods never leave their makers alone. Because people put themselves in positions of dependence on their gods."[2] In other words, if you make a god, that god will eventually rule you.

A lot of gods are being used as substitutes for the Savior. Listen to what the apostle Paul told his contemporaries about the people he knew: "So I tell you this, and insist on it in the Lord, that you must no longer live as the Gentiles do [so how were they living?] in the futility of their thinking. They are darkened in their understanding and separated from the life of God because of the ignorance that is in them due to the hardening of their hearts. Having lost all sensitivity, they have given themselves over to sensuality so as to indulge in every kind of impurity, with a continual lust for more" (Ephesians 4:17-19).

That's what people were like then. Sounds familiar, doesn't it? That's because people are like that now. Surveys tell us that more than two-thirds of American adults believe there is no such thing as absolute truth. Unfortunately, almost as many who claim to be born again also believe that there is no absolute truth.

Finding Satisfaction When Life Disappoints

Had my family not found Christ when they did, or, for that matter, had I not heard the good news of Christ, would I be led today to believe that there is no absolute truth? I might be practicing a form of behavior that would prevent me from meeting the life-changing Jesus. Fortunately, other people realized that I had a spiritual need, and they wouldn't let me argue them into remaining silent about my need.

Believe God about the spiritual longing of others. That longing is real. It's there because God put it there. Even though as a new believer my faith was weak, I could depend on the more mature faith of others to help me. Even though I didn't know until later that my family had the same spiritual longings I had before I met Christ—and were fighting against those longings as I did—I know now from that experience and many others in the years since that a spiritual longing is there in everyone. All the created religious beliefs only prove that we are made for God. They prove that we will believe in something, even if it is only in our own pride of unbelief.

I am a spiritual person. But I need to know what to do with that spirituality. I need to find the "more" that I was meant to have. I want to be all that I was designed to be and put here to be. I want to come to the end of my life a spiritual winner. And you do too.

FOR REFLECTION OR DISCUSSION

1. In what significant ways have you changed since you first trusted Christ as your Savior?

2. What spiritual influence have you had on your family?

Because I'm Really a Spiritual Me

3. In what ways are you inconsistent? What steps would you be willing to take to change in these areas?

4. What idols do you see people worshiping? Do you have any of these idols in your life? If so, what will you do about it?

6

WHO LOSES,
WHO WINS?

THERE IS ONE OTHER story about my dad that shows the change that God brings and how much he does that goes beyond our own weak faith. It is a memory that I cherish not only for its personal impact on me but for the reminder from God that he will not do things halfway.

Dad died in church. He was there with my mother for a special evening meeting with a missionary speaker. When it came time to receive an offering for missions, my dad, with other ushers, walked to the front. The presiding minister turned to my dad. "Nelson, will you lead in prayer?" he asked. Dad did. Then the ushers took the offering. As they all stepped into the narthex, Dad handed his offering plate to another usher and fell over dead. A heart attack took him. Doctors said he was probably dead by the time he crumpled to the floor.

My mother was called out, and word came back into the auditorium where the speaker was just beginning his talk. He stopped. Then he said to the audience, "I want you to think about something. Two minutes ago this man was talking to the Lord in prayer; now two minutes later he is talking to the Lord face to face." No one who was there that night will ever forget it.

Who Loses, Who Wins?

No Anchor but Themselves

My family had moved to the winning side. They had found what Jesus called "the pearl of great price." But even as they won and are winning, still there are others—family and friends—who choose the opposite road. Some have looked at God and yawned. Others have looked at God and said no. A few have looked at God and said, "*I'll* be god to me."

These are the losers, and many of them are angry. They expected life to be good for them, but it isn't. Some thought they would change the world; they could not. Others thought that at least they could change their own personal circumstances; they could not. Still others thought they could change their own inner lives; they could not.

Sooner or later reverses have come for them all. Because they have no anchor other than themselves, they face emotional struggles and frustration, which in turn cause a reaction that says, "I'm losing, and it's all God's fault."

Yet God has been to them only Someone boringly remote or sometimes a curse word or a vague concept left to others to think about while they have concentrated on themselves.

All around us we see people who once hoped they would be winning but who now feel that they are losing. Life isn't what they had planned or dreamed it would be. They are on a slide that no amount of increased activity will correct, no extra borrowing to buy something new will change, no raging at the system will alter. The slide continues—it's a slide into greater self-centeredness even though that self-centeredness has already failed them. It is a worship of self even when

Finding Satisfaction When Life Disappoints

couched in admirable terms—like my family, my children, my spiritual self.

My Family—Another Religion?

For example, we see family becoming a center for many people. Too often it is a selfish center. When the highway department proposes a road in their neighborhood, their cry is, "What does this mean for my family?" If something happens internationally, the response is, "What does this mean to my family? How are our family interests affected?" Even daily newspaper editors have noted that for the last ten years people have been less interested in international news than they were in the past ("Who cares what happens over there?"). They prefer local news ("my parks, my street, my Little League teams, my schools"). Family, the attempt to find roots, as commendable as it is, becomes a center of focus that cannot substitute for God who gave us our families. It is a substitute religion that will not satisfy.

Adults say, "I am not going to repeat my parents' mistakes with my children." But those "mistakes" they don't want to repeat are measured by what they know now and their circumstances now, not what their parents' circumstances were then. They don't know that their parents had different lives, different resources, different situations. The reason they don't know that is that they measure everything against themselves, by where they live, by their circumstances.

Recently a film producer said to me, "It's hard to show generational differences in a film today because viewers want to project

Who Loses, Who Wins?

back from where they are now. They don't understand and won't accept where people were then." So this film producer has to draw a variable line between what was reality then and what people will accept as reality based on what they are experiencing now. He can't show the truth from "back then" if it doesn't fit with people's perceptions of truth as they understand it now.

"We won't be like our parents. Our children will come first," parents who put family first are saying. "I will give up my career for the children," says a professional mother. "I will not put work ahead of the children," says a dad. They want flex time, shorter hours at work, but not fewer hours in the health club or in doing other things that they want to do personally. "Our children come first," they say.

Parents who think they are sacrificing for their children may be in for a shock. Whenever children or anyone or anything becomes our reason for being, whenever God is replaced, even with "my children," a painful fall is coming. Family and children cannot be a religion. Yet for many, that's what their family has become. Even increased church attendance for many is based largely on "what this will do for my children." We hear, "'They' had better have a good nursery, Sunday school program, youth program for my children."

The fall will come when children do what children as individuals have always done. Children will filter through their own systems all they learn from parents, peers, television, and films, and what their genetic makeup from two to three generations back dictates. They will do what their parents who made them the center of their worship never expected. Parents will say, "I gave up my career for you." The child will reply, "I didn't

Finding Satisfaction When Life Disappoints

ask you to." Frustrated parents will say, "We gave you the best," as they watch young people go their own way based on their own choosing.

Generations of parents before us have handled this, but they had a focus, a center that was larger than their children alone. They had a bigger world, a faith in God that went beyond family; and as a result, they had more to offer their children. Their children were richer for it. And their center wasn't shattered if their children didn't do what they had planned for them to do.

Our Center, Our Focus

When we make ourselves or others our focus, we will lose. When God is the center, we win—no matter what happens to us, no matter how painful.

One day while I was teaching at a Billy Graham School of Evangelism, a young pastor came to me between my two class sessions. He said, "My wife just left me and went off with one of the men in our church." Then he added, "My four-year-old daughter has a brain tumor, and the doctors have told me there is nothing more they can do. And a few weeks ago my mother died of cancer."

I thought, *Such pain!* This isn't theoretical pain; this is pain with a face on it. Yet this young pastor, hurting so much, wasn't centered in himself or even his circumstances. He had a larger focus. He will make it through.

When I have a larger focus, then whether I win or lose isn't just for me alone. Though my life now and my eternal destiny is a result of my winning or losing, there is more to it than that.

Who Loses, Who Wins?

Focused Christians are salt and light in a community. Focused Christians are missionaries in the neighborhood, demonstrating the deep realities of belonging to and serving Christ. But Christians are not salt and light if they compromise. If we are no different from others and show by our lives that faith in Christ is a preference but not a life-changing relationship, then we lose and our community loses.

We lose because we miss out on what God wants for us. Life, abundant life, is offered to us but missed by us. Then like anybody else we struggle on without either the peace of God or the involvement of God in our lives. No wonder so few people in our communities have a clear witness given them. At best, they only have the news media accounts of political Christianity that cannot save, or the moral Christian teachings that cannot save. They miss the Christ who alone can save.

Our World Loses Too

If we lose because our center is not in Christ and if our families lose because our center is not in Christ and our communities lose because our center is not in Christ, then our world loses too.

In my basement office where I do my writing is a wall hanging with 2 Chronicles 7:14 on it: "If my people, who are called by my name, will humble themselves and pray and seek my face and turn from their wicked ways, then will I hear from heaven and will forgive their sin and will heal their land." But it isn't printed in English; it is printed in Russian. It was given to me as a gift when I was teaching pastors at a conference on evangelism in Moscow. This was before the fall of communism.

Finding Satisfaction When Life Disappoints

I have it on my wall because it is a reminder to me not only of what God says in his Word, but also that other Christians in other places see themselves as God's people too. And they are. Though we may be provincial in our thinking, God isn't. God has a much larger family than most of us know. And many of them understand faithfulness in ways that we do not. There is a focus, a centering, that God is honoring in their lives.

The majority of Christians in the world are no longer in the West. Western cultures are quickly becoming a backwater of Christian influence. We used to be leaders in the world, with missionaries going out from us to other places. This has changed.

But that's what we in the West must expect if we tend to be our own center and Christ is permitted only to be at the outer edges of our lives. Those elsewhere who are committed to Christ will take leadership of the church and will be an influence in their own cultures and elsewhere in the world. That this is happening is indicated by the greatest rise in martyrdom in world history. Believers are dying because they are there. They are faithful to Christ, and they are not silent about the Gospel.

These believers are dying as well because too many of us who do claim Christ are not supportive of them. We are silent. The brotherhood for many stops at our borders. For some, it never even reaches beyond their own church, denomination, or community. The concept of the larger body is ignored. And when the body is ignored, so is the Head.

So in our world we have Christians in developing countries living lives centered in Christ but being martyred in great numbers, and Christians in safe Western countries neither speaking

Who Loses, Who Wins?

for Christ nor living in any way that distinguishes them from their culture.

Who loses in this life? Who wins? The ones who will not follow Jesus lose. The ones who stop others from meeting Christ lose. But the ones who will follow are told, "For this God is our God for ever and ever; he will be our guide even to the end" (Psalm 48:14).

Those who help others meet the Master are given the blessing today that God gave through Aaron years ago. It is a blessing that has never been rescinded: "The LORD bless you and keep you; the LORD make his face shine upon you and be gracious to you; the LORD turn his face toward you and give you peace" (Numbers 6:24-26). The blessed ones win.

He Enables Me

Will there be rough times for the faithful follower who obeys God? Yes, of course. Does God take us out of the storms? Not always. Can we win even when outwardly we seem to have lost? The answer again is yes.

It is yes because we have God's promise to his people who are able to say with Habakkuk, "Though the fig tree does not bud and there are no grapes on the vines, though the olive crop fails and the fields produce no food, though there are no sheep in the pen and no cattle in the stalls, yet I will rejoice in the LORD, I will be joyful in God my Savior. The Sovereign LORD is my strength; he makes my feet like the feet of a deer, he enables me to go on the heights" (Habakkuk 3:17-19).

We can say that because it is true. And we can experience the assurance that Jesus himself emphasized, "And surely I am with you always, to the very end of the age" (Matthew 28:20).

We go through our lives the same way that we drive down a road. We move along, sometimes faster, sometimes slower. Sometimes, when traffic is heavy, we are even standing still. Sometimes others go ahead of us, and we make room for them, not being jealous because they are doing better or going faster or will arrive sooner. And sometimes we pass another because we are going a little faster.

We are not in this life to be driving down the middle, forbidding others to get ahead. We are neither jealous nor angry if we are forced to slow down for a while or even stop. Our focus is larger than that. Our center isn't in ourselves.

In the Old Testament, Achish has an interesting comment for David—and I believe God meant it also for us, or it wouldn't have been kept for us in Scripture down through history. Achish says, "Whither have ye made a road to-day?" (1 Samuel 27:10 KJV). Now that is actually a negative verse, because the literal translation is, "Where did you go raiding today?" But the King James version of that verse has a different meaning. It shows that we are to make a road, and we are to allow others on that road.

So using Scripture in the King James wording, we can ask ourselves and each other: "Where did you make a road today?" Where did you make a road, not only for yourself but for other people? Where did you make a road where others who might have more opportunity or other gifts from God can pass you by? The way we answer that gives a good indication of how willing we are to help one another join the family of winners.

Who Loses, Who Wins?

Who loses? Who wins? In Christ we all do because a transformed life does make a difference. I can come to the end of my
life with the assurance that I won. I can come to the end of my
life knowing that I helped others win too. I am different, and
being different makes a difference.

FOR REFLECTION OR DISCUSSION

1. In what ways are you seeing "family" being made a substitute religion? Is this happening in your life?

2. Are you being salt and light where you live? Think about
what you've done the past five days.

3. How big is God's family? Think of your own family heritage and the country(ies) from which your ancestors came. Do
you still have relatives or acquaintances there? Do they have
religious freedom? Are you praying for your Christian brothers
and sisters there?

4. How would you paraphrase Habakkuk 3:17-19, fitting it
to your situation in life?

7

DIFFERENT DOES MAKE A DIFFERENCE

SONIA WAS SUPPOSED to die.

First she wrote her obituary; then she gave her daughters the jewelry and other personal items she wanted them to have. She was only fifty-three years old. But her heart was failing, and the doctors told her it was too late for a transplant.

Sonia is my cousin. We are kindred spirits, close because we both came to faith in Christ at about the same age—the first to do so in both our families. Over the years, with our spouses, we have vacationed and had other good times together.

I saw her at her low point when she was near death. She smiled at me and said, "You have no idea how much peace God gives when you know you are going to die."

I put my arms around her and said, "Sonia, I probably won't see you again here. But it won't be long before I see you in heaven." Then I got in the car and cried for the next three or four miles.

But Sonia didn't die. None of us knew, as she waited under hospice care for the end to come, that her heart would begin to strengthen. And months later the medical people who thought she would die told her she was strong enough for valve replacement.

Sonia was ready for her journey through that valley of the

Different Does Make a Difference

shadow of death. But I've met so many others who are not like Sonia. They are not ready. What makes the difference? Why can one smile as she waits for death while another rants and raves at the "injustice" and cries in the night, "Why me?"

Dying is easier when life has made a difference. Sonia's life has made a difference. The faith that people saw demonstrated when she had her health was just as real when she didn't. Circumstances don't destroy a person who is deeply rooted in Christ any more than strong winds will topple a securely rooted tree.

I want to be like that. I want to know that I am a different person in Christ than I might have been had I not met the Savior. I want to have that extra something that Sonia has demonstrated—that faith in Christ that makes a difference in my living and will make a difference in my dying.

Life Isn't Always Smooth

At certain times in our lives, we sense that we have to trust God more than we have been trusting him. Our heads may tell us that there should be no ups and downs in the Christian life. In Christ all should be smooth, and our trust should be even, the same all the time. But that isn't so.

Life doesn't treat us evenly. There are times that are good for us, and our pathway is smooth. But usually not for long. We can be going along and life is good, our trust in God is pleasant and easy, when suddenly difficult times come, and we plunge into a long period of despair or depression or pain. We have already seen that it happened to great Christians like Charles Spurgeon and Charlotte Elliot and Joseph Scriven. Why should we

Finding Satisfaction When Life Disappoints

assume that it will not happen to us? Or if it has before, that it will not happen again?

I think about that. I'm not morbid about it, going around with a sense of foreboding, but I'm not naïve either. Tough times will come. That is when Proverbs 3:5 comes back to mind: "Trust in the LORD with all your heart." It is almost like a demand that we are to be making of ourselves when we repeat that verse. It is as if you and I are standing off saying to our own selves, "Listen! 'Trust in the LORD with all your heart and lean not on your own understanding.' Stop going back to your own attempts at figuring out what is going on; stop looking for answers within yourself; stop looking for a way out or a way around.

"Don't keep leaning on your own understanding. You can't figure it out anyway. 'In all your ways . . .'" That doesn't leave anything out. "In *all* your ways acknowledge him. . . ." (v. 6). That's when I am able to say with certainty, "I know that you are God, and I know that you have an understanding of what is going on that I don't have. I know that you control everything, and I know that there are no surprises with you. I acknowledge that."

When you and I do that, then comes the assurance: ". . . and he will make your paths straight." You can know that God is doing that. The day will come when we look back and say, "That was the right path. God did direct me."

Different Is What God Intended

That we should be different is what God had in mind for us when Jesus came. It was what the apostle Paul was talking about when he said, "If anyone is in Christ, he is a new creation;

Different Does Make a Difference

the old has gone, the new has come!" (2 Corinthians 5:17). When Sonia was ready to die, she did not want to leave her husband and daughters and friends, but she was at peace with God. She was already a new creation, and she knew where she was going.

And because she was a new creation, I knew too that I would see her again. That's not wishful thinking when a person is in Christ. That's a reality, a certainty that I know as I live and that Sonia knew as she was approaching death. Becoming a new creation makes a difference in the way we die because it makes a difference in the way we live.

Our Way or God's Way?

Most of us are slow learners about our lives, even those of us who know we have new life in Christ. We may see God do something marvelous in our lives, and we think we will never forget it. But the next time a problem comes along, we tremble and begin to wonder if God can handle that situation. We worry about it. We seem unable to remember that the last time we had a problem God handled things beautifully.

But God doesn't necessarily do things our way. We ask for miracles and then try to figure out for ourselves how those miracles can happen. Will God do a miracle this way? That way? The people who were following Moses in the desert did that too. They wanted a response from God but figured they already knew the only alternatives God had. They were wrong.

When they were complaining that the manna God had provided was boring, they said they wanted meat. God said,

Finding Satisfaction When Life Disappoints

"Okay, I'll give you meat—not just for a day or two but for a month. You will come to loathe it." Then Moses and his people tried to figure out how God would do it. Moses looked at what he knew—flocks, fish. "There's not enough," he said. But God replied, "Is the LORD's arm too short? You will now see whether or not what I say will come true for you" (Numbers 11:23)—and he sent quail.

That wasn't in the scheme Moses had. Moses had a limited idea of how God could provide, and he expected God to fit in with it. But God had his own idea. When God does a miracle, he does it his way, and his way is always better than anything you and I can ever figure out.

When I've needed miracles from God, I've had them. Sometimes they have been dramatic, sometimes not so dramatic. Today I have a collection of spiritual memories based on earlier miracles. I needed them in my earlier years as a Christian. By now I've learned that God will always be God and is not limited by my small view of what that means. I didn't know that in my earlier days as a Christian. Sometimes I needed to see a miracle.

Miracles for Me

When I knew God wanted me in Christian ministry and I switched majors at the university from pre-law to business to English literature, I lost credits. Those had to be made up the summer of my senior year if I was to graduate in time to make the entering class at the seminary. I needed a miracle. I needed God to do something. He did, and I've had that miracle to reflect

Different Does Make a Difference

on ever since. God was teaching me that the Lord's arm is not too short.

I needed four classes in my English literature major to complete my course work. I could take two in the spring, leaving two more that I would need to take in the summer. But I also needed to work full time to earn money. How was God going to handle all that?

During winter term I had to choose the two classes in my major field that I would take that spring—but which two? I didn't know how to choose the two for spring because I didn't know which ones would be offered in the summer term when the offerings would be fewer. I hounded the dean's office; I talked to the faculty. No one could tell me what courses would be on the summer schedule. So, like a blind man taking a stab with his stick, I chose two of the four required classes for spring term. Weeks later, the summer class schedule was posted. Only two courses would be offered that summer—the exact two that I needed!

Then the class times were listed. One class would be held on Monday, Wednesday, and Friday nights. The other on Tuesday and Thursday nights. Neither one was in the daytime.

I was working at the university bookstore then, and they were laying off people after the springtime book-buying rush. Weeks went by; I was never laid off. Then the manager said to me, "We are going to remodel the store this summer. Is there any chance you could work here this summer?" Then he added, "And we are going to start at 7:00 A.M. instead of 8:00 A.M. and quit at 4:00 P.M. rather than 5:00 P.M."

Then it hit me. Look at who is in charge! I had a full-time job,

Finding Satisfaction When Life Disappoints

and yet I had time to clean up after work, eat a sandwich, spend an hour in the library in study, and make a six o'clock class each night for the exact courses I needed. Only God could have arranged that! And I knew it.

That's what I keep pulling up on my mental monitor. That's what I have to review over and over. Those miracles of God must be kept fresh. Because if I don't keep calling back to mind how God handled difficulties in my life then, I will still wonder next time if he can do it again. I will still doubt. That's because I'm no different than the disciples, who saw firsthand the miracles of Jesus—and should have remembered.

Making the Connection

When those disciples were discussing among themselves the fact that they had no bread (Mark 8:18), Jesus said to them, "Do you have eyes but fail to see, and ears but fail to hear? And don't you remember?"

Then patiently, as though speaking to forgetful children, he explained, "When I broke the five loaves for the five thousand, how many baskets full of pieces did you pick up?" Don't you see it? That's what he was asking them. Don't you see it? That's what he's asking me.

They had eyes, but they didn't see. They had ears, but they didn't hear. They didn't understand.

"Remember how I fed all those people?" Jesus said. "Can't you put it together in your own thinking? There was enough, wasn't there?"

"Oh, yes."

Different Does Make a Difference

"Not only was there enough, there was food left over. When bread was needed, it was there, wasn't it? Can't you make the connection?" He's asking them, "Can't you go from there to where you are now today? Can't you see and hear and remember?"

I recall very clearly a similar experience, not with loaves and fishes but dinner on a plate in the kitchen of the seminary dining hall.

When I went to seminary, having just finished paying four years of college tuition, I had only the money I'd earned that summer. I even sold a coin and stamp collection that I'd been building from the time I was a small child. Before classes began, I was out looking for work and was able to piece together several part-time jobs. One of those jobs was waiting tables in the seminary dining hall. Waiters didn't get paid, as I remember, but waiters did get to eat. The problem was, more students were signed up to wait tables than there were meals.

An afternoon came when I had no money—none. And I wasn't scheduled to wait tables. That meant I would not eat that night. I prayed, trusting God that he would help me get along without the food. Then, a few minutes after I prayed, the community phone rang down the hall. It was a classmate asking me if I would be willing to substitute for him waiting tables that night. I did, and afterwards in the kitchen I ate dinner.

That miracle was as large to me as anything I'd read about in Scripture, including loaves and fishes. It was "my" miracle, no one else's. God did it, and I knew he did. He was saying early on to me, when I was young and vulnerable and learning, "Did you think I wasn't looking out for you?"

God could be asking that question of each one of us right

now, no matter how many years in the faith and how many experiences we've had. "Don't you see?" "Don't you hear?" "Don't you remember?" "Don't you understand?" "Can't you make the connection?"

God hasn't changed. "Don't you understand?" He asked his disciples. That's what he's asking us too.

A Measurable Difference

It makes a difference, this life of belonging to Christ. The world may accuse us of being pie-in-the-sky-by-and-by people, but they don't know what God is doing right now. The Christian life is about heaven, yes, but it is also about all that matters today. Being different does make a difference in our lives, this hour, this minute. It shows in different ways.

News magazine writers admit to the odd discovery that regular churchgoers seem to be physically healthier than those who don't bother with God.[1] They don't know why, but we do. Educators admit that the same kids who don't seem to be making it in secular schools have far better records when they attend religious schools.[2] They don't know why, but we know.

Marriages are more likely to succeed among converted people who follow biblical teachings than among those who do not, even though most Americans at least claim to believe in God. Claiming it and living it are not the same. Those who obey the absolutes of God have better marriages. Others don't know why, but we do.

Different does make a difference. We see it in people who show up on the job ready to work every day. The difference is measurable between those who bring on alcohol-based traffic accidents and those who do not. The difference is there between those who have healthy attitudes toward sex as God's beautiful gift as opposed to those who only know exploitation and using others to satisfy personal cravings.

Different makes a difference across the broad spectrum of life. It can't be legislated. We can't tell people to "be different." Christ in us makes the difference. Those vocal people who want to legislate morality don't understand what believers know—Christ makes a difference.

Christ gives new life, abundant life. He said so, and he has proved it: "I have come that they may have life, and have it to the full" (John 10:10).

We who trust the Savior are making a difference within our own culture because we are different. We don't criticize the culture we live in for not living as we do—how could they? We don't try to make people behave like us; they can't. Rather, we are bringers of the good news that in Christ people will be different, and different does make a difference. God wants that difference for us. That has been God's message throughout history.

A Model for Us

Apart from life is death. Apart from new life in Christ is eternal death. That death is the opposite of what we were intended to have. We can hear the pleading in God's voice when we read, "I take no pleasure in the death of the wicked, but rather that they turn from their ways and live. Turn! Turn from your evil ways!" (Ezekiel 33:11).

Finding Satisfaction When Life Disappoints

God knows that different makes a difference. He planned it that way. "Therefore, if anyone is in Christ, he is a new creation; the old has gone, the new has come!" (2 Corinthians 5:17). I know that myself; so do millions of others in every culture of the world.

Do we need further evidence of what God wants for us? We can do no better than to check the models in Scripture itself. Would you like a good model for life? A good example to follow? Someone you can pattern your life after? I'd suggest Hezekiah. At least, I would suggest the young Hezekiah.

Hezekiah became king when he was twenty-five years old. Scripture says, "He did what was right in the eyes of the LORD" (2 Kings 18:3). "Hezekiah trusted in the LORD" (2 Kings 18:5). Second Kings 18:6-7 says, "He held fast to the LORD and did not cease to follow Him; he kept the commands the LORD had given Moses. And the LORD was with him; he was successful in whatever he undertook."

This was true of his life: He clung to God, he kept the commandments, and God prospered him. He is an example to follow—a model of what God wants us to be. But even a good model can break down, and Hezekiah did. Hezekiah was God's man, an obedient man, a fulfilled and dependable man, except for later on. He made a mistake. He serves as a warning to us all.

When it was time for Hezekiah to die, he begged for a few more years. He should have stuck with God's timetable. Had he died, he would have been known forever as a man who did not depart from following God and who kept his commandments. Instead he lived long enough to produce a son, Manasseh, who was just the opposite to his father—a wicked king.

Different does make a difference in the way we live and the

Different Does Make a Difference

way we die, unless we begin to take that difference too lightly as Hezekiah did. So live your life. Cling to the Lord as Hezekiah did in the early years. Keep God's commandments. Do what's right in the sight of God. Follow the example of Hezekiah. And then, be content to go on home with God.

I would rather die at an early age than to live to an old age and have everybody wish that I hadn't. I want to make my next steps good ones and to live as Hezekiah did in the early days. And when it's time to die, to do so, not with a complaint, but with a great sigh of relief saying, "I made it."

FOR REFLECTION OR DISCUSSION

1. How are you different from what you might have been if you had not met the Savior?

2. In what ways do you find yourself still leaning on your own understanding? How can you change that?

3. How has God surprised you by doing things his way instead of yours?

4. In what new ways are you, as a believer in Christ, "hearing" and "seeing" what happens in the world around you?

8

Making Your Next Steps Good Ones

SLOWLY, DURING MY JUNIOR YEAR at the university, a conviction grew that I should stop my pre-law studies and prepare for Christian ministry. But I struggled with it; it wasn't what I wanted.

So I ran from the call. The president of a supermarket firm where I was working offered me a scholarship and a salary if I would study marketing and commit to a career with them. The temptation to do that was strong, so I tried a business major for one semester. But God's call kept getting stronger. I was becoming more miserable every day. I remember when I finally surrendered. It was a capitulation, a giving up, and I wasn't happy with God about it.

It happened one evening while I was studying my economics text and doing a poor job of it. I knew that I was going against what God wanted for me—ministry! But what could I do in Christian ministry, I wondered. Why didn't God leave me alone? My misery level was building. Then the surrender came. Angrily, I slammed shut my book, looked up at the ceiling, and spat out the words, "Okay, God, if that's what you want, that's what I'll do; but whatever happens, it's all your fault!"

Now, years later, it turns out that those words were a good prayer. I was so ready to blame God for the failure that I was certain was coming that now I can never take credit for any successes he has given. God has done some great things in and through my life, but I can't take credit for any of them.

My Plan or God's Plan?

Still, surrendering to what I knew God wanted for me didn't mean that all my steps from then on were good ones. Scripture says, "If the LORD delights in a man's way, he makes his steps firm" (Psalm 37:23). My steps weren't always so firm; sometimes they were stumbling. But God, I have found, will look past that.

With that call to Christian ministry came the conviction in my own mind that I needed to work with young people in the army as a chaplain. Where did I get that idea? I don't know. It just seemed to make sense. My brother was a chaplain's assistant during his military stint; maybe that's what made me think that way. I sensed the need to work with young people, and to me, at that time with the draft, that's where young people were—in the military.

So all the way through my theological seminary studies I thought chaplaincy. I talked of it so much that one of my classmates became a career army chaplain. When I graduated, I applied to the army. "Get some practical pastoral experience first," said the person I contacted. So I accepted a call to a small church in West Virginia. Surely, I thought, the military would be next.

At the church I pastored, no one knew of my thoughts about the army. I didn't say anything because I wanted to concentrate

Finding Satisfaction When Life Disappoints

on doing a good job while I was there. But one day, looking at an insurance billing, I noticed that they had me paying extra for a heart murmur. I didn't have a heart murmur, I thought. I was just nervous the day I had the physical. I went to a physician friend in our church and asked him to check my heart so that I could get rid of that added premium. He examined me. "Well," he said when he finished, "I can't tell you that you don't have the heart murmur because you do."

"Oh," I replied. "Well, how bad is it?"

"It isn't bad," he said. "You can do anything you want." Then sitting back in his chair, he added, "Oh, you'd never be accepted in the military." And my world crashed.

All that planning and all that seminary preparation—how could I have been so wrong? Was God guiding my steps or wasn't he? If he was, how did I reach such a dead end, especially with a minor physical condition that God could have healed if he had wanted to? How could I believe that "if the LORD delights in a man's way, he makes his steps firm"? It didn't seem that God was taking much delight in me.

Yet in the months and years following, as I resigned myself to do the best I could where I was, God led in developing a youth ministry in that little town that brought many young men and women to Christ and others to a deeper life in the faith. Some are still faithful in ministry today.

It was as though God were saying to me, "I called you to work with young people. You're the one who said it had to be in the military. I never said that." From that time on, all the way into my years in campus ministry, God blessed the outreach to young people.

And God did something more. The year I became too old for military service, a doctor told me that apparently my heart murmur had disappeared. He couldn't find it. So far as I know, it has never returned.

Now What Is God Doing?

Will God make your next steps good ones? He has for me. Yet, like many others, I have not always gone along with God willingly. Struggle has been part of each step, and I have lived with the fear: *What if I turn the wrong way?*

These many years later I still live with a fear that I may be in the wrong place doing the wrong thing. It keeps me praying. I have seen God lead my steps. I have seen the good results of his leading. But today is a new day, so I keep praying.

When you and I want direction for our lives, we may not always be clear about it or certain that the direction has been given—even when we get it. That's not always because of weak faith. That may be just our human inability to know what God knows. God sees our tomorrows; we don't. Years of experience have taught me that God will probably leave me alone if I'm on the right path, but he will give me a good shove in the right direction if I'm not.

Experience helps me to understand that God doesn't have to redirect my steps if I'm already going in the right direction. Also, God doesn't have to keep reminding me, "Have you noticed; I'm leading you." That takes trust on my part. But I know that my trust can waver with my own confusion, my own perplexity over what God is doing now.

We're in good company. The apostle Peter was perplexed too. Peter, you will recall, received a vision, but he didn't understand it—at least not at first. Then some visitors came to help him, and it became clearer to him.

Remember that event in Acts 10:17? It reads, "While Peter was wondering about the meaning of the vision, the men sent by Cornelius found out where Simon's house was and stopped at the gate." He was wondering. That is often the way it is with us. We find ourselves wondering. The answers that will clear up the mystery are still on the way.

We want to know God's direction now. We want to have answers now to the problems we face. But answers usually come bit by bit. So while we wait, we are not always clear that we are getting those answers. That may be your situation right now. Some of the answers you need are still in process. You have some information, but you don't have it all. Only God has it all.

Sometimes our direction comes from others, as it did for Peter. Sometimes it comes through Scripture as we read a little further on in a particular passage. Sometimes, while we are engaged in something else, we suddenly gain the insight that we need. But it is all of God.

If you are perplexed, maybe about something going on in your life right now, remember that Peter was perplexed too. He was confused. Later on he saw it all fitting together, but not right then. How could he? God was doing something brand new. Peter didn't know then that God was about to turn a corner and take the Gospel beyond the Jews to the Gentiles. It would be a major change in the redemptive work of God. But Peter didn't know that. He'd had a vision, but he didn't understand it. The answer came bit by bit; and now, with 2,000 years of hindsight, we can see what God was doing that day when Peter had his experience on the roof.

Too Great for Your Lifetime

So even when you are perplexed or confused, God may be doing something through you that is the beginning of a major change. If he is making a major change or even a minor one, he will send further direction. Sometime later on you will begin to know. But even if you never know it all, God does. His timetable may be bigger than your lifetime. That's okay. Just be sure that you are willing for it to be okay.

Remember the great faith chapter, Hebrews 11? Scripture says of those heroes, "These were all commended for their faith, yet none of them received what had been promised" (Hebrews 11:39). They died believing, but they died without fully knowing everything. God was doing a work too great for their lifetime.

If that's the way it is for you, can you accept that? By faith can you take the steps God gives you even if you never see the results of those steps? Can you leave with God the results that may come to fruition years after you're dead? Do you have to know? Can you trust?

That's a tough decision for any of us to make. But it's a necessary one. We may not know all that God has planned, only that God doesn't waste a redeemed life. We may seem to be going nowhere; we may seem to be inconsequential. We may seem to be only occupying space. Our work may seem less important than someone else's. But that may be God's plan as he uses us for a future ongoing work that we may or may not ever see. The work of God didn't start with us; it will not end with us. We are part of a larger plan.

None of us is here by mistake. God knows who we are and why we are here. God got you started! Why should he quit on you now? If he brought you into new life in Christ—and you know whether or not he has—why do you doubt the work of God in your life now? God is steady, consistent, and faithful. That is why the apostle Paul, who faced far more trauma than most of us, could write: "Being confident of this, that he who began a good work in you will carry it on to completion until the day of Christ Jesus" (Philippians 1:6). God began it! He will perform it! God will someday complete it!

And notice again that it doesn't say just during your lifetime, but "until the day of Christ Jesus." Until Jesus comes to take you home or until he returns in a climactic end of history, God will continue to do the good work he has begun in your life.

Who's the Greatest?

You are part of a bigger plan—bigger than you, bigger than your circumstances, bigger than the events that influence you. God began the work! God will finish it! You can be confident of that, just as Paul was.

Let's go a step further with this. There is another part to these steps we take with God. And it's not an easy part to accept. God's bigger plan may call for you to have a smaller part in it than you would like. In fact, your part in God's plan may be very small.

How would you like to be told that you are going to be the

least of the least and the servant of everybody else? How's that for a calling? Are you prepared and willing to let others be famous or successful or wealthy (or whatever) while you are not? "Not me," you say. "I'm not going to be the least of the least. I'm not going to serve everybody else." Well, be careful!

Remember what Jesus told his band of followers? In Mark 9:35, we read that he called the Twelve and said to them, "If anyone wants to be first, he must be the very last, and the servant of all."

Or read the same thing in Matthew's gospel where Jesus says, "The greatest among you will be your servant" (Matthew 23:11). Not just the servant of God, but your servant too. The servant of you and me.

Some people will serve other people if they get something in return. They're always weighing the situation, thinking about what they're going to get back. It's like an investment. Jesus does not refer to them as great people.

But those who are really serving others have already been labeled by God. They're the ones he calls "the greatest." And people who think they're the greatest can tell right away whether they really are, because Jesus said, "The greatest among you will be your servant."

We've all met people who want to be first. We've all met people who want you to serve them. They want the most opportunities, the best benefits, the prominent place, and it may be given to them by others who are willing to be servants. I've met people who want perks and benefits for themselves and will walk over others to get them. I smile at that. I recall what Jesus said about people he saw who were drawing attention to themselves to earn people's praise: "They have received their reward in full" (Matthew 6:5). That's it! They've just had their reward—in full. What they want is what they get, but that's all. Jesus says there won't be any more for them.

Someday we're going to find that those who served are really first. Those who stepped back and took the lower places will find themselves being invited up higher. Those who were so impressed with themselves and even walked over others to be first will find that they are last. In that day both persons will understand the words of Jesus.

So it's not such a bad idea, is it—being last and serving everybody else? Think about it the next time an opportunity to serve comes along. Let God direct your steps. You'll have a satisfaction from serving that is rewarding now and will continue to be so. Those who want to be served don't understand that willingness. But that's because they probably don't understand the teachings of Jesus.

The next time you meet someone who thinks he's pretty great in the kingdom, watch him. See if he serves. That's God's measure of greatness.

Are you a servant? If so, God has already called you great. Do you think you're great? Then by definition you are a servant. That's the way God sees things.

A Time of Waiting

Your next steps—will they be good ones? Or is this a bad time for you? I find myself saying this a lot lately: "Hold on; things will change; it isn't over yet; God is still in control."

I say this to people who, like Rob, have just lost jobs, and they don't know what to do. I say it to people who have just had bad news about their health. I say it to parents who are trying to help their own children figure out life. And I find that comfort myself just as the psalmist David did. In Psalm 27 the psalmist is saying, "I am still confident of this: I will see the goodness of the LORD in the land of the living. Wait for the LORD; be strong and take heart and wait for the LORD" (Psalm 27:13-14).

David had a good perspective. We can learn from him. He knew that God is very much involved in the affairs of individuals. He also knew that God is not overwhelmed by a sudden bad turn of events or anything else that happens in people's lives, or in society, or in the nations. God is active for us within history, and yet he is outside of it. He is fixed, steady, secure when nothing else is.

You may be going through extremely shattering times right now. You may be feeling overwhelmed, wondering where to turn and what to do next. "Wait for the Lord." Waiting is not doing nothing, as some think; it's a concerted, proactive determination to trust God.

Life does turn corners, doors do swing open, things do change, and we can believe with the psalmist that "we shall see the goodness of the Lord."

Jesus helps us to understand this with an example. When you go out to your garden and plant a seed, after a while growth happens. How much influence did you have on that? There's a mystery to the growing of a plant from a seed, and there's a mystery to kingdom growth. There's a mystery too to the leading of God.

In Mark 4:26 and following are the words: "This is what the

kingdom of God is like. A man scatters seed on the ground. Night and day, whether he sleeps or gets up, the seed sprouts and grows, though he does not know how. All by itself the soil produces grain—first the stalk, then the head, then the full kernel in the head" (Mark 4:26-28).

How does it happen? Did you make it happen? Can you take a little seed and make a big tree out of it? The bigness is in the seed. God does a work in ways that we do not know.

You prepare the soil, you plant, you water, you go to sleep, you rest, you wait. You might get up in the middle of the night and say, "Nothing is happening." But then the seed starts to sprout and grow. Something was happening to the seed underground. You didn't see it. You waited.

We trust God to work with seeds. Can we trust Him to work with us?

There's a reason that this story was told by Jesus. You and I tend to be impatient. "Nothing is happening," we say. We look at our lives—nothing is happening. But maybe it's the nighttime. Maybe it's the time of waiting. What is God doing "underground," out of sight? If you can trust God when you place a little seed in the ground, can you trust God with what he is doing right now in your life?

Is Anything Impossible for God?

When I planned on the military chaplaincy, I thought I knew the best way to work with young people. As it turned out, the draft soon ended, and the real ministry was on the college campus where God eventually put me, first with students at Rutgers and Douglass in New Jersey and then at Michigan State University. God had to hold me back from the military chaplaincy to put me where He wanted me. He let the heart murmur do it. I wouldn't have understood if he had told me, "Things are changing; I have a different work for you to do."

Why is it that we think we can tell God what is right for us and what is not, what is possible and what is impossible? That's what I tried to do.

When the angel announced to Mary that she would become the mother of Jesus, Mary replied, "How will this be . . . since I am a virgin?" (Luke 1:34). In other words, that's impossible. It can't be. And within her human frame of reference, she was right. So convinced was she that it was impossible that the angel had to tell her: "For nothing is impossible with God" (Luke 1:37).

I have said what Mary said. You have said it. "That's impossible." "It can't be."

Is anything impossible for God?

I look at a seemingly hopeless situation, and I say, "There's no way out of this." "No way out for God," I say. But nothing is impossible with God. No thing. God is the God of the impossible.

What's the most impossible problem you're facing right now? Nothing is impossible with God, not even the biggest thing that troubles you.

Impossible? Good. Be glad it's impossible. Impossible for you, yes. Impossible for God, no. And when God acts, you'll know that he's the one who did it. You will have already admitted that you can't. If you just keep going on, step by step, God will make your next steps good ones.

Finding Satisfaction When Life Disappoints

Walking with God

Walking! Putting one foot in front of the other. Doing it prayerfully, trustingly. That's what we're called to do. There's nothing flashy about that. You don't break speed records as a walker, but you can cover a lot of territory and go on for a long time.

Steady walking, trusting God as you go—that's our calling. Walk like that, and you may not get the applause of the crowd, but you will get where you are going—where God wants you to be.

I have seen film portrayals of Moses parting the waters of the Red Sea so that the children of Israel could cross over. You know the scene with the Egyptians right behind them in their chariots. "But the Israelites went through the sea on dry ground, with a wall of water on their right and on their left" (Exodus 14:29).

They walked through. They didn't panic; they didn't rush and trip all over each other. They walked through. The Egyptians might have been right behind them, but they were able to walk through, knowing full well that God was doing something for them.

When the enemy is behind you, and you can feel him pressing in on you, and you are frightened and you pray, are you able to walk trustingly, knowing that God is doing a protective work for you, and you will be safe because he is in control? And do you find your footing firm because you are trusting him?

When you see a miracle of God in your life, are you able to go step by step in the strength of that, believing God as you

Making Your Next Steps Good Ones

place one foot in front of the other? There is a lot of faith to faith, a lot of trust in trusting.

Maybe in this business of letting God make my next steps good ones, the best way to make the most of every opportunity is to stop trying so hard to make the most out of every opportunity. That sounds at first like a contradiction, but it isn't. Ephesians 5:15-16 says, "Be very careful, then, how you live— not as unwise but as wise, making the most of every opportunity, because the days are evil."

Make the most of every opportunity, but don't rush here and there in frantic activity, trying to go farther than God wants you to go. The next best step for you might mean taking some quiet time alone with God, listening to him, getting some new direction, being refreshed. The next step for you might be making payments on your spiritual debts. That is one way you can make sure that your next steps are not only good ones but the best ones.

FOR REFLECTION OR DISCUSSION

1. What evidence do you have that God has been guiding your steps?

2. How can you know that you are on the right path now?

3. What does it mean to you that God may be doing something in your life that is bigger than your lifetime?

4. Look at the greatest problem you are facing right now. Is it too big for God? Why?

9

MY BEST DEBT

THERE ARE PEOPLE TO WHOM I owe a great debt. My friend Russ who first sowed the seeds of the Gospel that took root in my life. A Sunday school teacher who brought me to commitment to Christ. A doctor who told me I couldn't be a military chaplain. And there was another doctor, a missionary, who helped me when I hit an emotional wall that I couldn't climb over by myself.

We were living in New Jersey then, working with students at Rutgers University and Douglass College, pastoring a church that was struggling. The work never ended; there was no closure. No matter how much I did, there always seemed to be more than I could do. Gradually at first, then more quickly, I began an emotional downhill slide.

The day came when it was all I could do to leave the house for meetings, maybe teach a little, put together some kind of sermon for Sundays. The rest of the time I sat and stared. Sometimes hours went by, and I didn't even know it; I was lost in a fog of my own confusion. I knew I needed help.

A missionary doctor home on furlough was living only a few hundred miles away. I called him, and he invited me to come see him. I did. That night at his house he didn't just talk to me; he prayed for me. He laid hands on me and prayed. Then I went to bed and to sleep. When I awoke in the morning and started the drive home, I was a different man. I knew it.

Does God always work like that? No, not always. But he did

then. Healing continued. I could work again, and also I began to take graduate courses in counseling at Princeton Theological Seminary. God used those classes to help me even as I was learning how to help others.

Now It's My Turn

I am in debt to those who have helped me; it is a debt to God who brought the right people to me when I had need. I am indebted to them. It is a debt I can repay now by helping other people as God brings them to me.

Scripture teaches me, "Let no debt remain outstanding, except the continuing debt to love one another" (Romans 13:8a). For me, that has to work itself out in several dimensions: I want to understand the gifts God has given to me so that I can use them for others; I never want to forget that my debt to others is great; the payment on that debt must never stop so long as I live; I will be able to give to others because first I have taken; I can dispense because I have received.

Jesus spoke of it in a practical way when he said, "For I was hungry and you gave me something to eat, I was thirsty and you gave me something to drink, I was a stranger and you invited me in, I needed clothes and you clothed me, I was sick and you looked after me, I was in prison and you came to visit me" (Matthew 25:35-36).

Many people are obeying Jesus and giving like that, doing what he asked them to do in wonderfully creative ways. They inspire me to keep on with my giving. Others have brought hope to me. It is my turn to bring hope to others. I have a debt to pay.

Finding Satisfaction When Life Disappoints

Jesus could have been looking at the people around me, at my community or yours, in the descriptive Matthew 9:36 text that reads, "When he saw the crowds, he had compassion on them, because they were harassed and helpless, like sheep without a shepherd." Those kinds of people are all around me. I see them on the street—distressed, downcast, like sheep without a shepherd.

When I was in my state of depression or near depression, I couldn't do much. My inner self seemed to be shutting down. Yet the pressure to do more was pushing at me, making my condition even worse. I felt I could never do enough; the work of ministry was always pressing. That was defeating me. Even as I knew I needed to do more, I was doing less and less as my mind shut down. I'd either stare at the walls or sleep.

We think we have to do it all when we see the distressed, the downcast, the sheep without a shepherd. But we don't. We *do* have to pray for workers to help. Jesus said to his disciples, "The harvest is plentiful but the workers are few" (Matthew 9:37). He didn't tell them that they had to do all the work themselves. He said, "Ask the Lord of the harvest, therefore, to send out workers into his harvest field" (Matthew 9:38). Pray for workers!

God raises up the workers. He'll send them out. In our praying, though, he may say, "All right, I'm sending you too." But if he does send you, he will provide the power. It's his work, not mine or yours.

Look around you at the distressed, the downcast, those sheep without a shepherd. Pray that the Lord of the harvest will send out workers. Workers are useless unless they are sent, so pray that they'll be sent. Pray that there will be many, because Jesus is right—the harvest is plentiful! Be one of the workers.

My Best Debt

People in Darkness

My indebtedness includes reaching out to people who haven't given anything to me or to the church. They may be takers, they may be abusers, they may be criminals, but I have a debt to pay to them too. There's a description of people written two thousand years ago that could have been written this morning about the people we know. They are the words of Zacharias, the father of John the Baptist, inspired by God to foretell Messiah's ministry: "To shine on those living in darkness and in the shadow of death, to guide our feet into the path of peace" (Luke 1:79).

People were in darkness then. People were sitting in the shadow of death. They still are. We know people who are sitting in darkness right now. Right now they are in the shadow of death. They are without spiritual hope. And because they have no spiritual hope, they become depressed, sometimes suicidal. All life long they have depended on themselves, only to find that there's nothing there. They sit in the shadow of death. They're in darkness. They have been in darkness, they are in darkness, they will continue to be in darkness—unless we bring them to the Light.

That first-century message still holds, because the people described then were the same as people today. You know them. I know them. And God sends his message of hope to them because God knows them too.

Depression and spiritual and emotional difficulties are hard, and people need our help. They do not need condemnation. Even when people do things that bring on their own problems, we are still ambassadors of hope to them.

When I needed help, God sent two men to help me along to

Finding Satisfaction When Life Disappoints

saving faith. When I needed help, God sent a missionary doctor to help me. And even now as I give to others, I still need the help of other people. I'm not in this life by myself. I don't face my battles alone. I need the body, the church. I need the direction and the accountability that the fellowship of believers offers. That's why God gives us to each other. We *all* have debts to pay.

Debtors to Others, Debtors to God

Each morning during a Billy Graham crusade, team members meet together to pray. It's a rich time, a special time. I wouldn't miss it. Team members pray for the crusade needs, and they pray for each other.

There is good reason to do that. It's a scriptural reason. The apostle Paul told Timothy, "I urge, then, first of all, that requests, prayers, intercession and thanksgiving be made for everyone" (1 Timothy 2:1). In those team prayer sessions the needs to be prayed for are listed—people, situations, problems, joys for which to give thanks; and each person comes away spiritually refreshed and eager for the day.

Scripture urges that prayers be offered for everyone. That doesn't leave anyone out—not the difficult person that you don't like, not the self-centered person who doesn't pray for others, not even the person who rejects you and everything you stand for. In fact, the most difficult people are probably the ones who need prayer the most. That's our ministry, and it's one of the greatest ministries we can have.

We are debtors. I am, you are. Debtors to others, debtors to God.

My Best Debt

I have written and taught in various parts of the world, and I have met people who feel they must do something for God in order to repay him. They feel they need to sacrifice something, bring a gift, make a promise, take some spiritual pilgrimage, deprive themselves for God. Yet they are always uncertain about where they stand with him, because, in fact, our debt to God can't be repaid.

The psalmist talks about that and gives insight about it: "How can I repay the LORD for all his goodness to me?" (Psalm 116:12). Then it is as if he stops and thinks about it. "What shall I do? What shall I give to God? What gift can I bring him?"

Then he continues, "I will lift up the cup of salvation and call on the name of the LORD" (v. 13). "That's what I'll do," he says. "If I really want to do something for God, I'll take God's offer to me. I'll accept his gift. I'll receive his promise. I'll believe in his salvation. I'll give back to God by believing him."

I have never understood why is it that so many of those who want to do something for God, at the same time don't want to do what God wants them to do—receive the salvation he offers through the Lord Jesus Christ. Why won't we lift up the cup of salvation? Why won't we take his outstretched hand? Why won't we receive his offering for us? Instead, I still hear people saying, "I have to do something for God."

The greatest gift I can give God is my own heart in response to his gift to me—salvation through Jesus Christ. What shall I give to God for all his goodness to me? I'll take his cup of salvation. Taking is the greatest love gift I can give. Then, though I'll always be in debt, it's the best debt I can have.

Because I'm a Debtor

Having accepted God's gift to me as my "payment" to God, I can then turn to others out of a debtor's stance and just give without trying to prove anything. Nothing else matters when I know I am a debtor. Knowing that takes away all the pressures of needing anything from people. Just as that missionary doctor didn't think, *I'm home for a rest period; I don't want to give,* neither do I have to think, *That person isn't my responsibility.* I'm free of that kind of attitude because I'm a debtor.

I'm also free from selecting, saying yes to this person, no to that one. Because of my debt to God, I'm free from deciding if or how I'll respond to this person or that one. I owe too much to God to do that. Rather my outreach, "Let no debt remain outstanding, except the continuing debt to love one another" (Romans 13:8a), is an overflow of the grace given to me by the one to whom I owe my debt.

I am not the determiner of when to help another or the determiner of when to stop helping. God is, and I am to obey him trustingly. I tend to grow impatient; I want to quit. But my debt—the love coming to me from God—won't let me quit. Patience with people is difficult. Bearing with somebody, especially a person who just keeps messing up, is painful. I want to turn my back on him. Forgiveness is hard, but I'm a debtor.

The apostle Paul knew that, and, as God gave him the words, he knew what to tell us about that debt we owe and the compassion that needs to come from us to others. He said, "Therefore, as God's chosen people [and if we are in Christ, we have been chosen of God], holy and dearly loved [what a position—we are considered holy; we are beloved of God—and here come the instructions], clothe yourselves with compassion, kindness, humility, gentleness and patience" (Colossians 3:12).

Having that heart of compassion isn't automatic. When we get up every morning, we are not automatically dressed. We have to put things on. Well, you and I have to put on a heart of compassion too. Think it through; be aware of what you are doing. Then put it on. Compassion just doesn't happen. A heart of compassion has to be put on. That's what the apostle is telling us.

Additional Repair Work

The apostle goes on. But before I comment on what he tells us, I have to say something else. Remember that when I was converted my attitude changed. My sister said I was no longer easily provoked. She tried to make me angry, she says, but I was different. Well, I was, but not totally. Some of that anger began creeping back in after I became a follower of Christ.

My tongue began to get the better of me. I don't mean swearing or anything like that. I mean sharp remarks, cutting comments. I knew it was happening, and it began to get worse. So where was my heart of compassion if I could slice people apart?

Fortunately, God doesn't stop after his initial job on someone. He did some additional repair work on me.

It happened at a prayer conference. I realized that the speaker there that week had something that I didn't have. So one evening I made an appointment to see him. He heard me out and then became my intercessor. He prayed for me and helped me to pray for me.

Finding Satisfaction When Life Disappoints

God did a second work on me that night and took away that cutting tongue that needed to be dealt with. Does it come back? It has from time to time. But I received help when I needed it, and now I can go on, giving back to others and to God without the crippling effect of a sharp tongue.

Now, having said that, I can look at the rest of what the apostle taught. He told us to also put on kindness, humility, gentleness, patience. Because of our debt, we can be kind and gentle and patient, even with the same person over and over again. The apostle says, "Bear with each other and forgive whatever grievances you may have against one another. Forgive as the Lord forgave you" (Colossians 3:13).

How often does God forgive me? That's how often I am to forgive others. Has God had reason to turn his back on me? Does he have reason to say, "Oh, I give up. You'll never learn"? Could he easily say of me, "I gave you another opportunity, and look what you did with it"? He certainly could.

"Forgive as the Lord forgave you." That's what Scripture teaches us debtors.

Let's Talk About Money

Let's talk about another debt. This one may be more delicate because it is about money—our assets. This is where people get their backs up and say, "It's mine." But it isn't.

I work hard for a paycheck, but if I lived in parts of the world that I've visited, I'd have to work fourteen- to sixteen-hour days just for enough to buy food for one meal. So I can't say hard

My Best Debt

work makes money mine. Others work harder for less. What I have is a gift. I'm entrusted with it. But I cannot say, "It is mine."

I save, but so would others if they had it to save. My place of birth, the education I received, the opportunities to work that I've had are all out of my hands largely. I happen to live in a place where such benefits are possible.

So what is my debt to others? Most of the missionary sending countries are no longer in the wealthy West, yet we have the resources that many of those sending countries don't have. Do I have a debt to pay? You would think the answer is obvious to Christians, but it isn't.

I know a man who is a Christian who has had a great influence on others. He has done a lot of good. But in his latter years, he became so possessive of his money that he became more and more of a miser and a recluse. He was fearful that somebody might take his money away from him or expect him to share it.

Hebrews 13:16 instructs us, "Do not forget to do good and to share with others, for with such sacrifices God is pleased." But such Scripture is lost on this man, who himself was once an effective teacher of the Bible.

I knew this man when his income was increasing. He thought that God was giving this extra money to benefit others. But then the more he got, the more he accumulated through investments and interest, the less he thought of others.

Now he lives alone, just him and his money. There is no one with whom he wants to share anything. Someday he will die, and the money will be left to others. How much this man could be blessed if he would share it now.

Finding Satisfaction When Life Disappoints

Begging for a Chance to Help

Have you noticed that those who are poorest often give the most to help others, and those who are richest often give the least? Why is that? Maybe because the poor are so grateful for everything they have that they want to share it. Perhaps the rich think they have earned it themselves and don't need to share it. Maybe it's because the poor know what it is like to be poor, and they want to share what they have to help others. And maybe the rich, not knowing what it is to be poor, always think of themselves as still not as rich as they would like to be, and so they hang onto what they have.

In any event, Jesus noticed a widow who gave two coins. He also noted, with a different feeling, the rich man who gave to be noticed but didn't sacrifice at all. The apostle Paul too noticed that the poor were giving liberally. He said, "Out of the most severe trial, their overflowing joy and their extreme poverty welled up in rich generosity" (2 Corinthians 8:2).

The people he was talking about were in deep poverty, yet they were most "wealthy" in their liberality. The Scripture goes on to say that they actually begged for a chance to give and help.

How liberal are you in your giving? Do you understand your role as a debtor? If you are not extremely liberal in your giving, maybe it is not because you don't have very much (which is what we like to say) but rather because you have too much. If those who have the least tend to give the most and those who have the most tend to give the least, maybe we ought to pray, "Lord, make me poor enough to want to give." Now that would be an interesting prayer.

Whether it be a lot or a little, we have what God has given

us, and it isn't just for us. Whether it is money, our time, or an arm around the shoulder to comfort, "Do not forget to do good and to share with others, for with such sacrifices God is pleased," Scripture tells us (Hebrews 13:16).

With such sacrifices God is pleased. Are you pleasing God today? Will you please God tomorrow?

"I Know You"

Your reputation is a debt too. It's a different kind of debt, but it is a debt. We owe the church and the world a good reputation.

When I go somewhere, and someone introduces himself to me saying, "You don't know me, but I know you," that startles me. The person then explains the circumstances. Perhaps because of my nightly radio broadcast. Perhaps through my writings. Perhaps the individual has been in one of my writing classes or in a church where I have taught or preached. In any event, such a statement from someone is disconcerting to me. A person saying, "I know you," brings up negative thoughts as well as positive ones. What does that person know about me? What have I done? What mistake did I make that he or she is aware of? Where have I failed?

The apostle Paul also ran into the reputation fear. When he was explaining to the Galatian Christians about the early days, he said, "I was personally unknown to the churches of Judea that are in Christ. They only heard the report: 'The man who formerly persecuted us is now preaching the faith he once tried to destroy.' And they praised God because of me" (Galatians 1:22-24).

I wonder if that second part was a sigh of relief. "They praised God because of me." I wonder if Paul was thinking, *They are probably bitter toward God because of me. They may be turned away from the faith because of me.* He must have been pleased and relieved that they were glorifying God because of him.

How is it with you? Do you think you have no reputation? Do you think you live only to yourself? Do you think you are not known beyond your immediate circle? You are being watched, and I am too. And each time somebody comes to me and says, "You don't know me, but I know you," my first thought is, *I hope they are glorifying God.*

A Debtor's Checklist

The checklist of the debts I owe goes on. Even if I didn't have my own checklist of debts, there's one in the Bible. I know that you know it's there. We referred to it earlier—Jesus' statement: "For I was hungry and you gave me something to eat." When I read that, I have to check myself. Have I done that?

"I was thirsty," he said, "and you gave me something to drink." Did I?

"I was a stranger and you invited me in." And I check myself: Have I done that?

"I needed clothes and you clothed me." If I did that, when did I do it?

"I was sick and you looked after me." Have I done that?

"I was in prison and you came to visit me." And I check myself.

Jesus explains, "Whatever you did for one of the least of these brothers of mine, you did for me." Jesus is checking.

Read down the checklist in Matthew 25 and ask yourself, as I

My Best Debt

have, "Am I doing that?" A person wrapped up in himself won't do it. Even the person wrapped up only in his theological correctness may not do it. But the person who follows Jesus will do it.

What is my best debt? It is taking from God. It is giving to the work of God. It is helping the people God has called me to help. That debt won't ever be fully paid. But I can start where I am, with what I have, and work on my debt.

I owe a great debt because for me Jesus paid a great debt. I could not redeem myself. But having been redeemed by God, I am a debtor to all because God still loves this world.

There are a lot of people who need forgiveness and deliverance, just as I did before I was forgiven and delivered. Will I forget what I was? Will I lose touch with the lost because now I run only with the forgiven? Will you?

A lot of people in our world need mercy. They need forgiveness. They need what we have to give them. We have a debt that needs to be paid. And as we keep on paying, we will find with deep contentment that we still have enough. And, in Christ, enough is enough.

FOR REFLECTION OR DISCUSSION

1. What spiritual "debts" do you owe? How are you repaying those debts?

2. "Pray for workers." What does that mean in your situation, where you live and worship?

3. What is the greatest thing you or anyone can do for God? Have you done it?

4. Currently, what repair work is God doing in your life?

10

ENOUGH
IS ENOUGH

NOT LONG AFTER MY RECOVERY through the help of my missionary doctor friend, I wanted to go to Princeton Theological Seminary. Seward Hiltner, one of the best writers/teachers in counseling this century has produced, was teaching at Princeton Seminary when I started counseling studies there. When Hiltner joined Karl Menninger to edit *Constructive Aspects of Anxiety,* he concluded in his epilogue: "The empowerment needed for this confrontation can come only from God's grace."[1] I wanted that empowerment of God's grace in my life.

Pastoring in New Jersey made it easy for me to hop on the train once a week for graduate work at Princeton. I found myself not only in Princeton's classrooms but also doing clinical work at Trenton State Hospital. There in the training, sensitivity awareness sessions, and one-on-one encounters with patients, I learned not only about them but also about myself.

With the patients, in the classroom, and through other students, I learned who I was. Where once I had a feeling that there was something more and I was missing out, the same feeling so many people have, I came to learn that with God and through his grace, enough is enough. That's not a negative reaction to life's pains. That's a positive discovery founded on a deeper satisfaction in Christ. Enough is enough from God's perspective, and it is enough from my perspective too.

God himself is enough for me, and what he does in my life is enough for me. In him I find satisfaction in who I am. I have learned to recognize and celebrate my gifts, to enjoy my calling, to revel in my unique place in God's plan. There is genuine satisfaction in who I am, what I have, where I'm going, and what I can give to others. It is enough.

What About Tomorrow?

I have to ask you and anyone with whom I might have a conversation, are you satisfied with the way God is taking care of you today? Or are you too busy worrying about whether or not he'll take care of you tomorrow? In your life, is enough enough?

When Jesus fed a crowd with five loaves and two fish, ". . . he gave them to his disciples to set before the people. . . . They all ate and were satisfied" (Mark 6:41-42). Are you satisfied with what our Lord is giving you?

On that hillside Jesus kept giving. Everyone ate. They were satisfied. What he was giving obviously increased as he gave it out, because he started with only five loaves and two fish.

Each person had enough. Anyone being greeted at the door of his home that evening would have been able to say, "I've been with Jesus today. I've eaten, and I've had enough. Jesus fed me. I'm satisfied!"

Think about your own day. Have you had enough today? Has God taken care of you today? Or do you think you need more now because you can't be certain about tomorrow?

Finding Satisfaction When Life Disappoints

Can you trust God? These people whom Jesus fed had enough; they were satisfied.

"But," you say, "only for that day." They'd had enough, but obviously not too much. That is, it was not enough for the next day too. Certainly, those fish wouldn't have lasted overnight. Probably not the bread either—not in that heat. They'd be hungry again. What about tomorrow?

Well, what about tomorrow? Will Jesus be less the Son of God tomorrow? Will tomorrow's sunrise somehow have changed his power? Will God no longer be God? Will his love for you somehow be less, or will it disappear?

They had enough at that meal, and they were satisfied. As you trust God today, you're probably finding that you have enough and are satisfied too. Why then are you so worried about tomorrow?

Look at your resources. You had enough to eat today; you had relatively good health today; your family's love, your job security, your peace of mind was enough today. Did you know that yesterday?

Jesus asked his disciples, "What do you have?"

They didn't have much, but what they had was enough. You may not have much, and I may not have much, but Jesus wants us to take a look at what we do have. He already knew what they had, and he knows what we have too.

As Jesus fed that crowd, the disciples were allowed to participate in the miracle that day. And so are we, in our miracles, each day.

The crowd sat down; the food was distributed and distributed and distributed and distributed; it didn't run out. In fact, they had a lot left over to gather into baskets. The disciples, because they were giving what they had and because they saw what Jesus did with it, could help distribute; and they could say at the end, "Look what he did!" But they could never say, "Look what we did!"

We can't say that either, and that's the value in admitting, "I don't have much." Because when Jesus says, "What do you have?" and then does something wonderful with it, we can only say, "Look what Jesus did!"

Wealth Is So Uncertain

Jesus talked about birds having enough. He talked about God taking care of animals. He talked about the poor, and, though many people miss it, the Bible talks about the rich too. That's probably because the poor are more likely to say, "I have enough." The rich rarely say that. If, as Jesus once told people, it is as difficult for a camel to go through a needle's eye as it is for the rich to get into heaven, he must have had in mind the baggage that people, like merchants' pack camels, carry.

Is enough enough? How is it with you? Are you dissatisfied? Do you want a little bit more? Is the Scripture pointing to you when it says, "Do not store up for yourselves treasures on earth, where moth and rust destroy, and where thieves break in and steal" (Matthew 6:19)? And what about where it says, "For the love of money is a root of all kinds of evil" (1 Timothy 6:10a)? And what will we do with, "Command those who are rich in this present world not to be arrogant nor to put their hope in wealth, which is so uncertain" (1 Timothy 6:17)?

If you are rich, you had better not be conceited about it. Who gave you the opportunity to earn your wealth? Who gave you the mind to work things out in your business? Who gave you the ability to do what you do? Who placed you in circumstances where you could do it?

So don't be conceited about your riches. And don't fix your hope on the uncertainty of those riches. Remember this—your riches can disappear as fast as they came. Scripture is clear: "But to put their hope in God, who richly provides us with everything for our enjoyment" (1 Timothy 6:17b).

Enjoy It and Thank God

God does give all things richly, abundantly, and we are to enjoy them. It's God's loving care that causes him to do that. Don't let people tell you that we are not to enjoy what God gives us. He gives us all things to enjoy. If he gives you something, enjoy it. Take it for what it is—God's rich supply to you. Enjoy it and thank God. But you are not to be like a child at Christmas with too many presents, tearing open the packages, never saying thank you and then wailing, "Is that all?" Enough is enough. "Be content with what you have" (Hebrews 13:5), we are told.

God gives, and with the giving comes a call to responsibility. The apostle, talking to the rich, says: "Command them to do good, to be rich in good deeds, and to be generous and willing to share" (1 Timothy 6:18). So if you are rich, be rich in good works. Be generous and ready to share your riches. Your riches aren't just for you. If you have wealth—wonderful. Be generous. If you aren't generous, you will answer to God for it. Or, as in the parable of the talents, God may decide to place his riches in other, more generous hands.

Richer or Poorer?

Jesus told the story of a man who paid all of his employees the same wage—those who went to work early and those who went to work late—the same salary for all. Jesus could just as easily have made his story about those who work long shifts at low pay and those who work the same or fewer hours but with much larger paychecks.

But the point Jesus was making is summarized in his words: "Don't I have the right to do what I want with my own money? Or are you envious because I am generous?" (Matthew 20:15).

"That's it," says the corporate leader who misunderstands the message and justifies his own high pay and the low pay of his workers. "God gives me more because he is generous!" Well, be honest. Why would God do that? Why the generosity to you and not to another? What would happen if you took a cut in pay in order to raise the wages of the lowest-paid worker in your company?

The story that Jesus told is about more than wages. It is about spiritual gifts—God's gifts. If I work all day at a set wage and am paid that wage, I have no complaint. If someone else works only an hour but is paid the same, I have no complaint. I was paid no less than was agreed upon.

If I am invited late to the kingdom's work and I receive the same blessings as one who served the Master for many years, who is the winner? Who is the loser? If I heed the call to "come work in my field" early in life and I have a lifetime of service, am I richer or poorer? And if one hears the call "late in the day" and has only a short time to serve, is he richer or poorer?

Would I prefer fewer years in the Master's field, fewer years to serve? Do I envy someone who never had the chance to give his whole life to the Master's service?

The call of God is unusual. If one responds and God chooses to give that person the same gifts he gives another, that's God's choice. If one person has an all-day gift and one has a one-hour gift, that's still a gift. "Don't I have the right to do what I want with my own money?" he asks.

This is not an excuse, a justification for one person to have high wages for himself and low wages for others. This is a story about God's generosity in the spiritual realm. If I have a full life of kingdom work and another has only a short time, that's a blessing for me. We miss the point if we complain or are jealous of another person. If I understand the spiritual blessing of a lifetime spent serving the Master, would I want to add more to my reward and subtract from another person's reward? If by my estimation another person comes late and seems to be receiving too much, and I work all day and seem to have no more, I've missed the point.

Godly and Contented

God can do as he wills with those enlisted in his cause. We are his; we're not our own. It isn't our place to say, "But in my opinion you've been more generous with him than you have been with me."

Enough Is Enough

We look around at other people, but we need to be looking at the Master. He's the one who gives, and as the giver, he has a very big heart. "Is it not lawful for me to do what I wish with my own?" he asked. Yes, it is.

Or "are you envious because I am generous?" he asks. We're not to look at each other. We're to look at God, the giver of every good and perfect gift. With him, enough is always enough. The question is, is it enough for you? In Christ, are you contented? In Christ, can you declare, "Enough is enough"? If you can say that with contentment, you are called a godly person. I have to believe that if you can't say that, the opposite label fits. You become an ungodly person.

The apostle Paul told us that godliness is great gain when accompanied by contentment. The two go together. Some people are quite godly, but they are not very contented about it. Some people are contented, but they are not very godly.

After the apostle says, "For the love of money is a root of all kinds of evil," which many people have memorized, he adds, "Some people, eager for money, have wandered from the faith and pierced themselves with many griefs" (1 Timothy 6:10). Not too many have memorized that!

The discontented, the people who have got to have more, tend to wander away from the faith. The love of money, the worship of it, the striving for it, doesn't give contentment and doesn't give godliness. Instead it takes us further and further from the faith. Those people hurt themselves and then wonder why they are so miserable. "I have more money than I ever had, but I'm miserable," they say.

Then we find a person who doesn't have much but is godly,

and we realize that he is contented. We recognize that that person has great gain.

So what are we going to pursue? Godliness and contentment? Or will we fall in love with money and, in pursuing it, pierce ourselves and be in constant pain? God doesn't want us to be miserable. He wants us to be contented. Contentment comes from godliness. That's the greatest gain.

Are You Desperate Yet?

Years ago I heard a story. I don't know who first told it; it may have been old by the time I heard it. No matter. It was new to me, and I have never forgotten it.

The story is about an older man and a younger man walking along a path, and the younger man asked, "How can I find God?" The older man didn't answer. After a while they came to a stream that they had to cross. As they were wading across, the older man put his hands on the head of the younger man, pushed his head underwater—and held him there. After what seemed a very long time, he let go, and the young man came up sputtering and gasping. He cried out, "What did you do that for?" Quietly the older man replied, "When you want God as much as you wanted that air, you'll have him."

Are you desperate yet? I don't mean physically; I mean spiritually. Scripture says, "For he satisfies the thirsty and fills the hungry with good things" (Psalm 107:9).

If you want God's goodness, how desperate are you for it? A lot of us would like all of God that we can get, but we really don't have that deep longing, that soul yearning for him. It is the longing soul that God satisfies. It is the desperate soul that God fills.

If we sing, "Fill me, Lord . . ." and don't really mean it, nothing happens. If we say, "Satisfy me, Lord," and that is just a glib off-the-cuff remark, we remain empty. The soul's longing for God is like hunger; it is all-consuming. When you are truly hungry, you can't think of anything else.

Are you hungry for God's goodness? When you are longing for something, every thought is a part of that longing. If you want that longing satisfied, open your soul to him.

Psalm 107:9 is a good promise for days like this: God "satisfies the thirsty and fills the hungry with good things." There is a lot of longing these days. But there is also a lot of satisfying and filling that God wants to do and is doing. Why should you not have what he wants for you?

I know now what I want. I want what God promised his people through Ezekiel when he said, "I will give them an undivided heart and put a new spirit in them; I will remove from them their heart of stone and give them a heart of flesh" (Ezekiel 11:19).

That's what I want—an undivided heart, a new spirit, a heart of flesh instead of stone, a heart soft toward God, not hard toward him. I want the Spirit of God renewing me, a heart focused on him, undivided. I don't want to go back and forth from being contented to being discontented, going first in this direction and then in that direction.

An undivided heart. That is enough. A tender heart. That is enough. A heart in tune with the Spirit of God. That's what I want. That is enough.

Finding Satisfaction When Life Disappoints

God loves me. Since our Lord promised that if we ask for anything in his name, he will do it, I'm going to ask for an undivided heart. God loves you; what are you going to ask for?

FOR REFLECTION OR DISCUSSION

1. How are you learning to celebrate who you are and the gifts God has given to you?

2. Are you able to say with contentment, "I have enough"? Why? Why not?

3. What does godliness with contentment mean to you?

4. What does it mean to have an undivided heart? Do you?

11

GOD LOVES ME

THE INVITATION TO become a campus chaplain at Michigan State University was exciting. The year was 1967, a time when students were protesting U.S. involvement in Vietnam, a time of campus unrest and the Jesus movement. Before I moved there, I was told I could complete my graduate studies because Michigan State University offered a program in counseling similar to Princeton's. My credits from Princeton would transfer. So that summer I moved from New Jersey to East Lansing, Michigan, and that same summer M.S.U. canceled the program I needed. There I was with half of what was required for a degree and no way to complete it.

But that was another doorway, a way God used to tell me I'm loved. Even more than that, it was a way to help me show confused students that they are loved too.

I discovered just how economical God is. All the classes I took at Princeton transferred to upgrade my 1961 seminary degree to an M.Div. But also the counseling material I'd studied prepared me to work with students during those troubled times. Over the next six years, men and women came to strong faith in Christ, and many are serving in Christian ministry today. God knew what I needed. The studies I had done were exactly right for the times.

God Loves Me

Then people around me, including family, counseled me to work toward a graduate degree in journalism since I liked to write and had already started publishing. I did, and it gave me the ability to teach through magazine articles and then books about what God was doing among that day's youth, who would someday be labeled the Boomers. And when the campus began to quiet down in 1973, it was because of my writing that an invitation came to move to *Decision* magazine. Two and a half years later Billy Graham invited me to succeed the retiring editor. I served as editor of *Decision* for more than twenty-one years—telling millions through the pages of the magazine about the love of God.

Nothing Wasted

Why does this tell me that God loves me? Because there were long nights during that time when I wasn't sure what was happening. Why had God started me in a graduate program at Princeton if he knew I couldn't finish it? Why had the counseling program at Michigan State been canceled? Why did I arrive on campus just as unrest was sweeping across the nation's campuses, with demonstrations, bombings, the shootings at Kent State, and the student riots at the Chicago Democratic Convention? Why was I studying journalism at a graduate level, sitting in seminars with editors and publishers? How could journalism, theology, and counseling ever fit together? What was God doing?

I didn't know; I could only keep going. It was only later that it all began to fit together. God was showing me, "I love you," "I have you in my control," "Trust me." God, in his economy, wasted nothing in those years. He used every part.

Finding Satisfaction When Life Disappoints

God wanted my obedience; he wanted my heart, just as right now he wants yours. Is God directing your heart? When Paul was writing to the Thessalonian church, he said, "May the Lord direct your hearts into God's love" (2 Thessalonians 3:5a).

Then he added another point to that: "and Christ's perseverance." His perseverance! Is your heart moving in that direction? Can you picture your heart actually moving closer and closer, more into the love of Christ? Will your heart really be happy anywhere else?

The Eyes of the Lord

One of the Scripture verses I memorized a long time ago says, "For the eyes of the LORD range throughout the earth to strengthen those whose hearts are fully committed to him" (2 Chronicles 16:9a). I memorized that text because it helped me. I have found in this Scripture a word of comfort, a word of warning, and a word of reconciliation.

We don't have to live very long before we realize that life can take some sudden changes. A news bulletin on television, a phone call in the middle of the night, a pathology report, and everything changes.

God knows that. He is not taken by surprise. He is there. He sees. There in Chronicles, tucked away in this book of history, is that word from God to comfort us. Verse 9: "For the eyes of the LORD range throughout the earth to strengthen those whose hearts are fully committed to him." The *New American Standard* version phrases it, "For the eyes of the LORD move to and fro throughout the earth that He may strongly support those whose heart is completely His."

Do you realize what that means? God is not like us. His eyes are moving all the time to support strongly. He knows what is happening to us.

When the disciples were in a boat, the sea got rough. They thought they were going to drown. They thought Jesus was off somewhere in the hills praying. He *was* praying, but the Bible says he saw them. Jesus saw that they were distressed, and he came walking to them on the water. The disciples didn't know that he saw them. They might not have been so worried if they had known. He sees you and me too. He is aware when the sea we're in is rough and our little boat is about to be swamped.

And remember Moses? When he was leading the people out of Egypt, there were mothers, fathers, screaming babies, sullen teenagers, old people on crutches, cats, dogs. And Pharaoh's army was right behind them. Do you remember what the people said? Just what we might be tempted to say: "It's hopeless! Were there no graves in Egypt that you brought us out here to die?"

Moses' reply was, "Do not be afraid. Stand firm and you will see the deliverance the LORD will bring you today" (Exodus 14:13). He knew that God had His eye on them. Early on it was clear: "The LORD kept vigil that night" (Exodus 12:42). God was watching them and watching out for them.

You may be up all night worrying. God is up too—all night. He knows. He sees. He is watching.

Nothing is hidden from God. "The eyes of the LORD are everywhere, keeping watch on the wicked and the good" (Proverbs 15:3). God does see. We need to know that.

Finding Satisfaction When Life Disappoints

God Delights in You

The psalmist tells us, "The LORD delights in those who fear him" (Psalm 147:11a), which means those who respect or stand in awe of God.

The psalmist goes even further: The Lord delights in those "who put their hope in his unfailing love." He takes pleasure in those who wait for God's love, who are not trying to produce some spiritual force or strength or ability on their own. God favors the person who waits for his lovingkindness. Waiting is one of the greatest works we can do when that wait is for God's lovingkindness, a wait based on respect, fear, awe of him.

I teach at the Billy Graham Schools of Evangelism. Hundreds of pastors gather in different locations around North America for instruction. It is a rich and rewarding experience to teach the pastors at these schools. But more than teaching takes place. Healing occurs too. So many pastors arrive hurting, feeling confused, even wondering if they should stay in the ministry.

Ministers have said to me, "My wife has left me." The pain they feel is overwhelming. *Does God still love me?* is the unspoken question. "I was in seminary; my wife left me and took our child with her," one man said. "My wife is seeing another man," said another. It's a little-known problem because if a minister leaves his marriage, the scandal of it often makes big press. But when the minister's wife leaves him, and it seems to be happening more and more, there tends to be silence. Sometimes the church gathers around and is supportive. More often, it does not. These clergy need to know this unchanging truth: God still loves them; God delights in them.

Without Love—Nothing!

Often at weddings I hear readings from 1 Corinthians 13. I have heard it read so often that in some cases I think it has become too familiar, without meaning any longer. When I read those words thoughtfully, I see, "And if I have a faith that can move mountains, but have not love, I am nothing" (1 Corinthians 13:2b). That hits me hard.

"Nothing," he says. "I am nothing." Take the love out, and I have nothing. I am nothing, even if my faith is so great that mountains can be moved by my trust.

If God is love, and he is, and I have God, then I have love. But if I don't have love, then isn't it doubtful that I have God? And isn't that something I had better look into very carefully? Certainly I had better look into it before I quote 1 Corinthians 13 again.

Some think of love or compassion as being only a warm, fuzzy feeling. But God's love is tough, a strong love that comes even in the midst of anger and grieving. That was so that day when Jesus healed a man with a withered hand.

It happened in a synagogue on the Sabbath. Here was this man with a withered hand. The religious leaders were watching to see if Jesus would violate the Sabbath by healing that man's hand.

Scripture doesn't say that Jesus looked at the man who was ill. Rather, it says, "He looked around at them . . ." (that is, at those who tried to stop him), "and, deeply distressed at their stubborn hearts, said to the man, 'Stretch out your hand.' He stretched it out, and his hand was completely restored" (Mark 3:5).

The religious leaders wanted to trip Jesus. They weren't

interested in the man who was hurting—only in the Law. Jesus was angry and grieved about that. He was angry because they were so legalistic; he was grieved because they missed the point of God's love and care. They didn't understand God's compassion toward the person who had such a need. They didn't understand how important people are to God.

I've met people like that, people who try to stop good works—love, compassion, healing, care—because they don't know about the love of God. We have to hold them off so that we can do the good that we know God wants done. Some people see only the Law and don't care about others. Our Lord understood the Law, but he also saw the person. So do the people who follow Jesus; they know that God loves, God cares.

Your love for people comes from a spilling over of God's love to you. Because you know God's love, you have lots of love to give to others. If you didn't know God's love, you wouldn't have much to give at all.

Decide to Love

Joshua was talking to his people. He said, "You are to hold fast to the LORD your God" (Joshua 23:8a). Hold fast to him. He didn't say we only need to have nice, warm, gooey feelings about God. We are to cling to him. That's a decision we make.

Joshua goes on, "So be very careful to love the LORD your God" (Joshua 23:11). He uses the word *love*, yes, but adds "be very careful to love." That's more than a feeling; that's a concentration. We set our minds to it. We decide to do it.

But a warning follows: "If you turn away . . ." But I'll let you read that in Joshua 23 for yourself. I'm interested right now in the part that says, "Be very careful to love the LORD your God." Be careful, pay attention, decide to love God.

We look at ourselves and say, "Self, you need to love God." You need to make that a priority. You make a commitment to do that. Concentrate on it. There's a whole lot more to loving God than just how we feel inside. It is a decision we make to love—heart, soul, mind, and strength.

Who loves me? If I were one of those pastors who has lost his wife, I could not say that my wife does. If I'm one of those parents who has lost his children to drugs or some other rebellion, I could not say, "My kids do." If I'm one of those people who feels rejected and hurt by others, I couldn't say, "Society does." But I can know with certainty that God loves me. I can say it because in his Word God keeps telling me that over and over again. That is the one fixed certainty in a life where nothing else is certain. That certainty holds me even though, like most everyone else, I have to admit that in my life I've made some good choices; I've made some bad choices.

FOR REFLECTION OR DISCUSSION

1. How has God been "economical" in your life?

2. Think about the most recent storm you've gone through. What is the evidence that God saw you and helped you in that storm?

3. Is God delighting in you? How do you know?

4. In what way is clinging to God a decision that we make?

12

I'VE MADE SOME GOOD CHOICES; I'VE MADE SOME BAD CHOICES

ONE AFTERNOON IN A little cafe in Annapolis Royal on the Bay of Fundy in Nova Scotia, two women sat in a booth talking. One said to the other, "I've made some good choices; I've made some bad choices. But I'm fifty-one years old now. If anything is going to happen in my life, I have to make it happen."

I didn't mean to overhear their conversation, but I did. And I realized, that woman is not alone. We who think like that are everywhere. For most of us, life isn't turning out the way we wanted it to. We tend to think as she thought, *I have to make it happen*. But even if she tries harder, can she really make something good happen in her life? Can any of us? At some time or other haven't we all tried?

The longer I live, the more I realize that I can't fix all that is wrong with our world. I can't fix other people, and I can't fix myself. As I read about others before me, people who have struggled with honest questions about themselves as I have, I find my struggle isn't new. Five hundred years ago, Thomas à Kempis said that we can't make others as we wish them to be, and we can't make ourselves as we wish ourselves to be. And he was right. We can't.

My life is a process of trying to make things better—for me, for others. There are the good choices I make; there are the bad.

I've Made Some Good Choices; I've Made Some Bad Choices

Sometimes I think about the good, and I feel pleased about myself. Other times I think about the bad, and I don't feel so pleased anymore. As the years pass, I realize that I can't always make good things happen. Most of us know that, even though pop psychology people are pitching their slogans and programs, trying to tell us that we can make good things happen in our lives all the time. I can't do it.

But I've learned that saying, "I can't," isn't a mark of failure. Saying, "I can't," isn't a resignation to defeat. Saying, "I can't," makes me then ask, "Who can?" And that is the first step to my answer. It is God who can. Simple? Silly? No. Saying, "God can" is neither simple nor silly.

God can repair and finish. God is the one who says, "For my thoughts are not your thoughts, neither are your ways my ways" (Isaiah 55:8). If they were the same, how could he help? If they were the same, I'd have no hope. I'd be at my wit's end. Despair!

God is the one who says, "Call to me and I will answer you and tell you great and unsearchable things you do not know" (Jeremiah 33:3). God knows what I don't know. More than that, he knows me better than I know myself, and he knows my tomorrows as well.

God is the one who doesn't change. "I the LORD do not change" (Malachi 3:6a), which means that all that he ever was, he still is, and all that he ever promised will still come true.

God is not incomplete but complete, total. Though I can't complete what is incomplete about me, God can. He is the Divine Completer. Have you found that out yet?

Not Like Me

God isn't like you and me, always looking back at yesterday, recalling what was. God doesn't spend his time looking at our bad choices, our mistakes. He isn't saying, "You made your bed; now lie in it." He isn't out to keep us down.

I think back now on some of the poor teaching I gave our children when they were little. I think I tended to communicate that God is beyond pleasing; God is tough, even demanding. I think I must have taught that idea because I was often that way myself.

Because I was a tough disciplinarian as a father, it would have been easy, even unavoidable, for my children to think, *God is looking at my mistakes. God doesn't say, "Well done." He says, "You could have done better."*

As you and I talk with other people, we find many who are bruised, battered—people who are still trying to please, who are convinced they cannot ever do enough or be good enough. They may be trying to please parents—even parents long gone—or God. Why do we do that? Isn't God saying, "Please let me help you"?

God's promises, as real now as they were when they were given, encourage me. First, I listen to what he tells me about the past: "I will repay you for the years the locusts have eaten" (Joel 2:25a). Then I listen to what he tells me about the future: "So do not fear, for I am with you; do not be dismayed, for I am your God. I will strengthen you and help you; I will uphold you with my righteous right hand" (Isaiah 41:10). And finally I know: "... we may receive mercy and find grace to help us in our time of need" (Hebrews 4:16b). I'm being offered help! My choices,

I've Made Some Good Choices; I've Made Some Bad Choices

good or bad, are neither too big, too controlling, nor too overwhelming for God. Yours aren't either.

I know that what I've done with my life to this point—the bad choices I've made—have consequences that can't be corrected. The results of my mistakes will always be there. There are the injuries I've brought on myself, the destroyed relationships, the poor educational choices—these remain. I see a good example of that in the life of Esau. His choice influenced not only his own life but the course of history. Selling his birthright in a single weak moment because he wanted to satisfy an immediate craving wrecked his life. Our choices do have ongoing consequences.

I meet another person, Samson, who learned that too. He had a special strength that came from God. But he chose to play fast and loose with it because of the weakness he had for Delilah. He thought playing around with the gift God had given him wouldn't matter, that he could always go on as he had before. He couldn't; he lost. And you can think of others like that.

But even those kinds of choices with all their consequences do not have to ruin you or me. God still has the last word. "'For I know the plans I have for you,' declares the LORD, 'plans to prosper you and not to harm you, plans to give you hope and a future'" (Jeremiah 29:11), he says through the prophet Jeremiah. That was said for our encouragement.

Educated Guesses

But will I ever know that hope; will I ever have that future? Will you? Like that woman in Nova Scotia, will we keep on thinking that we are the ones who must "make the good happen"? If I won't admit that I can't, that only God can, I will probably continue to face despair. You will too.

If we stubbornly refuse God's offer of help, we'll probably continue to be the victims of our own weaknesses and, unfortunately, the victims of our own foolishness. But you and I can change direction. Each of us can say at last, "I will let God step into life's struggles with me. I will claim his promises." It isn't a guess. It's a reasoned decision. Guessing may work in business but not in matters of the soul.

In our office, when it is budget-planning time, we find ourselves asking a question: "What is this going to cost next year?" Sometimes we don't know. Yet we can't afford to make some wild guess. So we look at previous years' budgets, ask ourselves questions, and then make what is called an educated guess. That usually works in business. But spiritually speaking, when we are dealing with God, the term "educated guess" may be an oxymoron.

Some people try to make their own educated guess about God. They say, "Sure, I feel there must be a God. I believe, sort of." But that educated guess comes from themselves, their own thinking. They have no input from outside themselves. They haven't read God's Word for themselves. They don't know what God is revealing about himself. They haven't had a personal experience with God. They don't talk with people who do know God. So theirs is a guess.

When we are people of uncertainty, people who only guess about God, then what we conclude about God is not even an educated guess. At best it is a wild guess. People who guess

I've Made Some Good Choices; I've Made Some Bad Choices

about God and then find they have guessed poorly, that "their god" doesn't work out to their satisfaction, tend to give up on God—or so they say. Only they haven't given up on God. They never had a relationship with God to give up. What they gave up was their own wild guessing.

The person who makes his own guess about God doesn't have a foundation to build on. Why would any of us think that we can run our lives on the basis of guesses? Spending a little time with the words of Jesus shows us that we can't.

The Danger of the Idolatry of Self

Jesus knew that one of the biggest forms of idolatry is the "idolatry of me." "I can take care of myself," I say. "If I don't look after me, no one else will," I declare. "If I don't do it, it won't get done."

Jesus answered those kinds of statements. Scripture says, "To some who were confident of their own righteousness and looked down on everybody else, Jesus told this parable" (Luke 18:9). He then told the story of the man who reminded God about how good he was: "I'm not like other men—I don't do evil things, I fast, I give tithes." So this is a specific story told about a specific kind of person, the person who trusts only in himself.

But near that man was another who didn't keep on saying, "I, I, I." Instead he said, "Lord, be merciful to me, a sinner." Jesus told us which one went down to his house justified. It wasn't the one with "I" trouble. It was the one who stood off, didn't look at anybody else, looked only at himself, recognized his sinfulness, and confessed it.

Finding Satisfaction When Life Disappoints

I know a lot of people who trust only themselves, never God. Probably you do too. In fact, most who say they don't believe in God treat themselves as though they were God. Have you noticed that those who say they don't believe in God are usually the same ones who blame God for any negative thing that happens to them? They follow their own ways, not God's ways, get themselves into trouble, then curse God for the trouble they get themselves into. They put a most interesting spin on their thinking.

If the negative things that happen to people who worship themselves are always "God's fault," why don't we hear these same people thanking God for the blessings that come too? But they don't. When something good happens, they say, "Look what I did."

I hear people blaming God when they fall and bump their heads socially or scrape their knees financially, but I don't see them running from darkness to light so that they won't keep hurting themselves. If you're like me, you find yourself wondering how long it will take before they discover where all the dead ends are.

Looking for the Formula

One evening I was asked to return a telephone call to a man who lives in another part of the country from me. He had seen my name in print and thought I could help him. He said he was confused about God; he was fearful that he was going to hell. After listening to him for a while, I began to discover that he was the victim of a form of spiritual pride that holds that God

I've Made Some Good Choices; I've Made Some Bad Choices

can't or won't help him. But it wasn't God's help he wanted. He wanted God's agreement with his way of life. He claimed to have prayed, to have followed scriptural injunctions. "But nothing has happened," he said.

As I talked with him, he began losing interest. I thought, *Am I confusing him? Am I unclear? Am I not listening properly?* Finally he told me that he didn't like what I was saying because I was telling him the same things a Christian counselor had been telling him, and he wanted to hear something else, something different. He didn't want guidance or suggestions or admonitions from Scripture. He wanted me to give him a formula to follow, certain steps to take "that will work for me." His emphasis was "for me." He didn't want God to change him; he wanted God to make him comfortable while he continued living outside of a serious commitment to God.

This man wanted to feel better about his life, but he didn't want God to influence his life. He wanted to know that God would accept him into heaven without expecting a daily relationship now. He didn't want condemnation; he didn't want hell. He wanted some simple steps to follow in order to satisfy God. But he didn't want God adjusting his life. Deep down inside he seemed to be convinced that he was really quite fine; he just needed to be sure that God agreed with him, and he wanted to know what steps he had to take to be sure that God was agreeing with him. Basically he wanted God to adjust to him. He was the center, and God needed to come around and understand that. I couldn't help him.

As far as I know, that man is still struggling. That me-centered pride is insidious. It makes this man feel as if his seeking isn't going anywhere, and yet he won't back off from his self-centeredness. He wants God to help him but only on his own terms. He is making choices dictated by his own pain but ultimately prefers the pain to surrender. All the while he is asking, "Why doesn't God help me?" He may come to the end of his life like that. I've known men and women who have.

A Lifelong "No"

I once knew a man who spent his entire life stubbornly resisting the idea of choosing God. He refused to say yes to God's offers. And when he died, he died shaking his head no to the concerned request of his family that he think again about God. He held to a belief in self that shaped his life, even though the more his stubbornness ruled him, the more he hurt his career and his relationships. He became an unhappy old man. Yet he would not give in to God's beckoning.

I believe that death does not erase our awareness, and I think that person knows now what he should have done and could have done. But it is too late. It must be a terrible thing to spend eternity seeing our own life and all the opportunities we had to be what God could have helped us to be, yet knowing those were the very opportunities we refused.

I've found that nothing ever really dulls that sense of being incomplete, even while we are still too rigid to admit that we are incomplete. I think now, like the man spoken of in the Scriptures who made his own discoveries too late (Luke 16:19-31), this man who refused to submit to God would say to anyone who will listen, "Don't wreck your life just to prove to yourself that you can make choices without God. You are proving nothing except the reality of what Jesus so pointedly said to his own disciples—"'Apart from me you can do nothing'" (John 15:5b).

Pulling Me Back

All of us make good choices and bad choices. The ultimate good choice, the one upon which all other choices follow, is to choose to say yes to the one who can help us continue to make other good choices and to overcome bad choices when we do make them. God can wade into the stream of our bad choices, rescue us, help us out, and set us on a firm and better path. That's what God in his love does. In other words, none of us can stray so far that God cannot reach us and pull us back.

Love that pulls me back and pulls you back is there because God is there, and God is love. When I am hurting, I am not alone. When you have physical or spiritual aches, you are not alone. When we are groaning from anxiety and the torments of life, we are not alone. God is there with us. That's his assurance to us. Always, right to the end of life—and beyond.

Maybe in My Lifetime, Maybe Not

You and I can trust God to honor our faith in him even if we never see great results from that faith in our lifetime. We can believe God to answer prayer even if we die long before our prayers are answered.

One of the best-known passages of Scripture in the New Testament is Hebrews 11, the faith chapter, which lists the great

Finding Satisfaction When Life Disappoints

host of witnesses who have gone before us. We referred to it earlier in chapter 8. I find great comfort in that chapter. It begins with the words, "Now faith is being sure of what we hope for and certain of what we do not see" (Hebrews 11:1). Then it goes through a list of people who were faithful, and then comes that powerful verse 13: "All these people were still living by faith when they died. They did not receive the things promised; they only saw them and welcomed them from a distance."

I talk to people who tell me that they want to trust God with their choices. They do pray, but life is going on, and God hasn't answered, they say. They are becoming impatient with God. Isn't God hearing them? Or are they thinking that God has to follow their timetable? Are they saying, "Unless I see God answer prayer, he isn't answering prayer; unless God responds visibly in my lifetime, he hasn't responded"? Does that sound like something you've done?

Ask yourself the questions I have to ask myself. Can I believe that God is not deaf? Can I believe that God hears my prayers and that in his own time he is going to answer? Can I trust him enough to realize that maybe he has already answered and that where I am is exactly where he wants me to be, and what I am doing is exactly what he wants me to do, and no dramatic change has come because he doesn't want to change anything?

Is my faith such that I will trust only so long as God indicates in some tangible way to me that he has heard and he is responding? Does he have to prove himself to me? Does God have to prove himself to you? Isn't faith really what the Scripture says it is: "the substance of things hoped for, the evidence of things not seen" (Hebrews 11:1 KJV)?

I've Made Some Good Choices; I've Made Some Bad Choices

Can I believe that God is hearing and God is answering because he says he is? That is what marked those believers of old as men and women of great faith. Maybe that's the difference between them and some of us.

New Chapters in Our Lives

Each day God is writing new chapters in our lives. Knowing that, I can go on making choices, confident that they are good choices because I am yielding myself to him and obeying his Word and trusting that he does want good for me.

His mercies are new every morning, as the prophet Jeremiah discovered (see Lamentations 3:23). They are new for me because each day I'm seeking God anew. Yesterday affects today—of course it does—but today is a new beginning, or can be. God isn't bound by anything—past, present, or future. There is excitement in knowing that.

Will I still struggle like the woman in that little cafe in Nova Scotia? Will I still keep trying to make something good happen on my own? Probably. Will you? Probably so, but maybe a little less each day. Maybe we will begin to learn that what Jesus said about us is true: "Apart from me you can do nothing" (John 15:5b).

Talk to some who have spent their years trying to make their own lives work. Many will confess to a feeling of failure, a sense that nothing they have done in their lives has really mattered after all. But talk to those who seek to live each day under the control of the eternal Christ, and they will confess to an awareness that no matter what they have done, seemingly great or small, it was blessed by God, used by God, and has had an ongoing dimension to it. Christ is the Vine, and we are attached to the Vine; we are the branches. The life of the vine flows through the branches, and with the life of Christ flowing through us, we can do so much that matters and lasts.

"I've made some good choices and some bad choices," we say. But the choices that matter are the choices made in the attached-to-Christ mode. That must be why throughout the Scriptures God reminds us with stories and explanations, "It is you I care about." It is surprising and wonderful that he constantly assures us, "You are important to me."

When I first wondered if my family would ever be saved, God showed me. When I struggled with failures and closed doors and confusion about what was coming next, God showed me.

He not only showed me what he could do by doing it, but he also showed me himself—the one who does it. Over the years God has shown me a wonderful certainty: There is more for me even when life seems to offer less.

I know that now.

FOR REFLECTION OR DISCUSSION

1. Have you learned to say, "I can't"? What's the evidence?

2. In what specific way have you seen God repay you for "the years the locusts have eaten"?

3. How do you help people who have "I" trouble?

4. What new chapters is God writing in your life?

AFTERWORD

Have you too discovered that God offers more when life offers less? Tell me about it. Write to me in care of the publisher. I'd like to know your story. And if you have yet to discover the great truth of God's love for you, please write to me as well. I want to pray with purpose that soon you too will know.

ROGER C. PALMS

NOTES

Chapter 5

1. Samuel Moffett, "Why We Go: Recapturing our Motivation for Missions," *Christianity Today*, Vol. 38, No. 13, November 14, 1994, 54.

2. Bob Gudzwaard, *Idols of Our Time* (Downers Grove, Ill.: InterVarsity Press, 1984), 13.

Chapter 7

1. Joseph P. Shapiro with Andrea R. Wright, "Can Churches Save America?" *U.S. News and World Report*, Vol. 121, No. 10, September 9, 1996, 46-53.

2. Kenneth L. Woodward, "Catechism Lessons," *Newsweek*, September 23, 1996, 62; Richard Lacayo, "Parochial Politics," *Time*, Vol. 148, No. 15, September 23, 1996, 31-33; John Leo, "A Challenge the Schools Didn't Take," *U.S. News and World Report*, Vol. 121, No. 12, September 23, 1996, 32.

Chapter 10

1. *Constructive Aspects of Anxiety*, ed. Seward Hiltner and Karl Menninger (New York, Nashville: Abingdon Press, 1963), 161.